Wild Woman

A Daughter's Search for a Father's Love

Sandy Cathcart

NEEDLE ROCK
PRESS

Visit Needle Rock Press at www.needlerockpress.com

Visit Sandy Cathcart's Website at www.sandycathcartauthor.com

Visit Bill Miller's Website at www.billmiller.co (not a typo. Leave off "m")

All of the above can be found on Facebook.

Wild Woman

Needle Rock Press
2395 C Ashland St., PMB 444
Ashland, OR 97520

Needle Rock Press books may be purchased from booksellers or by contacting sandycathcart@gmail.com

Needle Rock Press books may be purchased in bulk for ministry purposes by contacting sandycathcart@gmail.com

ISBN-10: 1943500037
ISBN-13: 978-1943500031 (Needle Rock Press)

for
Dad and Momma

because of
Creator Redeemer's grace our story is just beginning

On His wings I have soared
Under His wings I have found refuge.
He has taken me from the valley below,
High on a mountaintop, drawing me closer...
Drawing me closer to Him.

—*Robyn McMullen*

Contents

Part One

Shadows and Sighs

If you could see His face
I know you would love Him.
His beauty far outshines the sun.
If you could hear His voice,
No other sound would thrill you.
He is the ONE who gave the SONG.

—*Sandy Cathcart*

1

Tracking Home

I know His Voice.
He is all I want.
He is all I need.
When I call on Him,
He answers me.

—Debbie Rempel

October 7, 2009, Wednesday evening
Dad's hospital room

Rain plasters the windows of my father's hospital room, blurring the world outside until the buildings and trees look twisted and misshapen. I sit on a hard bench with my arms folded across my chest braced against the cold.

Everything in me wants to run from this place, to escape to the wilderness, back to the land I know and love, away from these beeping machines and antiseptic smells, away from the tube that runs down my father's throat and keeps him alive. Yet, my being here is necessary—first to affirm that life is precious, but also because I am a broken woman in search of healing for myself in these last moments of my father's life.

A torrent of bad water has passed beneath the bridge between my father and me, and I've been focusing on that

3

turbulence for far too long. I know my first step in crossing that bridge is to put away bad memories, but the more I try not to think about them, the more they come to mind. I have a lot of questions I would like to ask, but it doesn't seem right to be dwelling on bad memories when my father cannot speak in his own defense.

"God, please help me think on the good," I whisper.

When I turn from the window, Dad's eyes are open, staring at me.

"Hi Dad," I say, and then I continue the endless deluge of words. "Remember when we were headed to Sawyers Bar . . . ."

1954
Fort Jones, Northern California

When I was seven years old traveling with my father on the back roads of Northern California, I had my first encounter with a mountain lion. Its fur was as black as the inside of an abandoned well. Dad called it a panther, but there were no panthers in our area—or so we were told.

We were nearing Sawyers Bar when the panther fell off the side of the mountain. It was about the size of a full-grown man and landed right in front of our truck. It must have hit something on the way down, because it lay there in an unmoving heap. My dog and best friend, Nipper, went wild with barking and lunging at the windshield. Dad stopped our old pickup just in time to avoid running into the lion.

"Stay in the truck, Sandra," he said.

He didn't have to say *that* twice.

With Nipper barking frantically in my ear, I watched as Dad squeezed out of the truck, closed the door with a snap, and walked over toward the crumpled black form easily seen in the light cast by our headlights.

Panther. Just the sound of the word on my tongue conjured up horrifying mental images of young children being dragged from their beds into the jungle. It didn't

4

take much imagination to envision the panther grabbing Dad and dragging him into the thick forest, leaving Nipper and me alone. I wasn't sure which would be worse—to see Dad taken off by a crazed panther, or to be left alone to face Bigfoot. One thing I was sure of: that Bigfoot *would* come if Dad was dragged away, and Nipper was no match for him.

Dad had just passed the left headlight, causing a big shadow to spread across the road, when the panther sprang to its feet!

I never saw Dad move so fast. He went one way and the panther went another. Dad was around that truck and back in the driver's seat before the panther's tail disappeared into the darkness. Nipper jumped in my lap, pawing at the passenger window and barking madly.

Dad and I talked of little else for days. Everyone thought we were crazy.

"There are no panthers in our woods!" neighbors kept insisting.

But it was hard for them to argue when Dad pointed me out as an eyewitness. I reveled in my high standing for as long as I could. It wasn't often I received my father's praise.

I was raised an only child, and the three years we spent on a thousand-acre ranch between Fort Jones and Etna in Northern California were my happiest. We moved there from Camp Pendleton where Dad was a corporal in the Marine Corps. It was quite a change from a small trailer perched on a sandy beach where I attended a military school that began every morning with a shouting rendition of the Marine hymn.

Our Northern California home was a small house with white-washed walls hidden in a forested valley and surrounded by farmlands where leather-skinned cowboys drove herds of cattle down single-lane highways. In Fort Jones I attended a school where grades one through six gathered in three rooms and we "borrowed" trash can lids to slide down a snow-covered hill at recess.

A big yellow bus transported me to school and back. On the days when Momma wasn't at the road to greet me, I would sneak across the neighbor's field when the meanest bull was looking the other way. That bull terrified me but, in truth, he was probably harmless. He always waited until I was almost to the far gate before he made his charge. Then he would head butt the gate with a tremendous blow.

When my heart calmed, I would brave "Spooky Wood," a small section of forest that remained hidden from the sun both day and night. It's interesting that I was afraid of Spooky Wood when it was no more than a small patch of forest. In contrast, I never experienced fear while roaming the twelve hundred acres of thick forest and hidden valley that sheltered our house. That was always a safe place for me. I suspect it had something to do with the fact that Nipper was my faithful companion on the ranch.

Nipper and I were a team. I considered him my protector, unless he was off chasing something else, which was about half the time. He was part wolf, which meant he had a lot of things to chase. I'll never forget the day we brought Nipper home. It took two grown men with big poles to hold Nipper's wolf mother back while Dad reached inside the pen and retrieved Nipper as a pup. By the time he was two, he had silver fur and long legs like his mother and the golden eyes and pointed ears of his German shepherd father.

The summer before my seventh birthday, Dad gave me a snakebite kit and taught me how to tell time and direction by the sun. After he and Momma were convinced of my wilderness survival skills, they let me roam through the forest as carefree and fearless as any wild animal.

While Dad was off driving truck or working as a mechanic, I roamed through the forest searching for animal friends. One time I talked with a coyote. We met in a small clearing on the northeast side of our ranch. He sat very still, just a few feet away, staring at me. I wasn't very tall back then, so we were nearly eye to eye.

He was probably sizing me up for dinner, but at the time, I thought we were friends. Standing in one spot, just as my father had taught me, I cooed over the coyote in quiet words, nearly whispering.

"You're beautiful," I said. "Look at all your pretty silver fur."

The coyote cocked his head, first left, then right, as if weighing the truth of my words. I've nurtured a bond with wild animals to this day. In fact, I feel more at home with animals than I do with most people. That bond has earned me the name, "animal magnet" by my closest friends.

Our small home was miles from the nearest town, and our only electricity came from an old generator we fired up on Saturday afternoons. We used it to run the wringer washing machine during the day and to light the house for company in the evening. The grownups would play cards while we kids pounded each other with feather pillows.

October 7, 2009, Still Wednesday evening
Dad's hospital room

"Remember those days Dad? Those Saturday nights were about the only time you would find me indoors."

Dad's eyes are closed. My endless words must have soothed him back to sleep, but my mind is captured by those good memories of three wonderful years wandering through the forest.

I still prefer the outdoors, but I've remained indoors now for over a week in my father's hospital room. He entered this place after a sudden attack of pneumonia. His lungs had improved and the doctor was checking him out to return home when something happened to Dad's heart and he ended up here in the Critical Care Unit.

Sometimes the urge to flee this place has fallen on me so strong that I've made it to the door—at others to the parking lot. Once I even drove down the road, heading to the mountains, only to turn around and return to the hospital. My family celebrated Dad's eightieth birthday earlier this year. He looked healthy enough to be with us for a long time, but eighty is a difficult age to face a life-and-death battle.

I cannot escape the madness of this battle, because I cannot bear the thought of my father walking through the valley of the shadow of death alone. Momma feels the same way, but her body is too weak to spend more than a few hours at a time with him, which means I am here as much for my mother as for my father. She was 17 when she married Dad, and they've been together for 62 years. I can't imagine how she will survive without him.

So I remain here on the hard bench that runs along the wide window and I watch silent Rambo movies with Dad while I talk, talk, talk, and he says nothing, because the tube forbids him to do so. I break only for a meal or two, usually in the middle of the night when I stand in the cafeteria and wonder whether my last meal was breakfast or dinner. Every moment runs into the next.

This moment I find myself staring at my father's feet so beautiful in their manicured whiteness. This is the first time I have noticed them. They are usually encased in work boots or comfortable house slippers. They are uncovered now, not at my father's request but because a doctor ordered it.

I despise this cold place where a strong man is at the mercy of strangers; some who connect and show great compassion; others who simply do their job.

It seems impossible that anything can change in our relationship at this late date. My father can't even speak, how can he tell me the words I long to hear? And even if he does, it seems unlikely that words will make much of a difference. For the past year, every time I left my parent's house, Dad would walk me to my Ford Explorer, lay his calloused hands on the frame of the open window and say, "You know I love you, don't you?"

But I could never answer. Hurtful images from my teen years were too strong in my mind. I tried to push them aside, but they kept popping back up. Images from later years piled on top until a river of hurt stood between me and freedom, keeping my tongue mute.

Now, as I wait over my father, I wish he could ask the question one more time. There are some things I would like to ask him in return.

The irony is also not lost on me that Dad's suffering has completely stopped my hectic pace. I'm enrolled as a degree student at the same college where I teach writing. The only reason I'm not currently teaching is because during the fall season, I work as camp cook alongside my husband, Cat, who guides for 4E Guide and Supply. I'm also self-employed in a business that involves writing, photography, and art. For the past year, that's been my father's other mantra. "You need to slow down," but I wouldn't listen. Sometimes I tried. I would stop a thing or two, for a day or two, but never for long.

I certainly have plenty of time now in these long drawn out hours. I've discovered I cannot read, cannot do anything that takes any kind of thinking power. Insanity threatens every dark moment. The river of bad memories floods my mind, creating a sense of despair so deep I don't even care to live.

I could crawl on that bed with Dad and just fade away.

2

Mountain Womb

Have you ever given orders to the morning,
Or shown the dawn its place,
That it might take the earth by the edges
And shake the wicked out of it?

—Creator Redeemer

**October 2009, Between Wednesday and Thursday
Dad's hospital room**

The night grows long, broken only by the quiet footfalls from a parade of technicians and nurses watching over Dad. They need only the light of a computer to see what they're doing. Green computer light makes their faces glow in the dark, like aliens from another planet. Most of their actions are rote, merely procedures they perform day after day and night after night.

I sit in the dark and think about the irony of my hectic pace plunging to an abrupt halt. I don't think this is what Dad meant when he cautioned me to slow down. I've lost my passion for life, can't remember why I should go on. All my busyness seems to be nothing more than the actions of a hamster turning its wheeled cage.

I'm walking a dangerous line, and I know it, but I'm just tired enough that I'm not sure what to do about it.

I'd like to talk with Cat, but he's in the wilderness. I'm supposed to be with him, cooking for our hunting clients as I do every October. Cat offered to stay with me, but I urged him to go, to keep the commitment I cannot keep. He's unreachable by phone, or by car. It would take hours to hike or mount a horse and ride in.

I wish he were here now; wish I hadn't told him to go. Yet, really, what could he do? My needs are spiritual. My help must come from God, the One whom I've come to know as Creator Redeemer, yet I find it difficult to hear God's voice over the beeping machines.

Dad is asleep for the moment, so I walk on silent feet through the doors of the Critical Care Unit and up the stairs to the hospital chapel on the third floor. Candlelight casts a soft glow as I slip into a pew and place my knees on the kneeling rail. I pour out my heart to the One who hears all. My brain registers the fact, understands that even a sigh directed at God is heard. Still, I wish Creator Redeemer would sit right here next to me where I can see his face.

"I live and move and have my being in you," I whisper, but at the moment I'm not feeling the truth of those words. I simply feel tired and worn and terribly alone.

Though the chapel offers a bit of quiet, it doesn't fulfill my need of revival. Wilderness has always been my place of connection with Creator Redeemer. I feel safe in the womb of the mountain.

September, 2001
Sky Lakes Wilderness, Oregon

"You sure you girls are going to be okay?"

I break into an enormous smile. "More than okay," I assure Steve.

Steve Evans shakes his head. He's owner of 4E Guide and Supply. Cat works for him as a guide and I work as camp cook. This current trip is a gift. Steve and his friend,

Mike Kaiser, have hauled a canvas tent, two cots, a camp stove and a mule's load of food and equipment across seven miles of wilderness to my secret place.

Mike is stretched out flat on a log; his cowboy hat covers his face. Sickness plagued him most of the way up the trail. "Wake me when it's time to get on the horse," he mumbles. He looks as if he's ready for burial. I help Steve string up my canvas tent between two trees while my friend, Tresa, finds a perfect spot for her pup tent a stone's throw away. I can barely pick out the tent's shiny green nylon through the thick growth of timber.

Tresa is the only person camping with me until Cat joins us on Saturday. Steve is worried about leaving us here, two women alone in the wilderness, but he should know better. Tresa spends most of her time in the outdoors, and I am more at home in the wilderness than anywhere else.

After Steve and Mike leave, Tresa and I start each morning together, then head off separately for our own adventures. Through five days of peaceful bliss I fulfill my vision quest, connect with the nighthawk and sleep under the stars. I entered the wilderness with questions, yearning to leave my hectic life behind and to make some sense of it. As usual, my questions change shape and morph into a sense of rightness. One by one, they fall away as I witness the symphony of creation shouting the presence of Creator.

Today the sweet scent of wild huckleberries fills the air as I make my way to Boston Bluff. I long ago dubbed the bluff my favorite spot in the Seven Lakes Basin. I often claw across the narrow ridge to a point where white rock plunges several hundred feet on three sides. I've taken Tresa out here twice a day, and she's grown to love it as much as I do. The music of Honeymoon Falls creates a wild melody, and off in the distance is the birthplace of the middle fork of the famous Rogue River. The Middle Fork carves a hard left at the bottom of Mudjukewis Mountain while Ruth, Ethel and Maude Mountains keep their vigil on the right. The rugged rim of Crater Lake stands in the distance with miles of healthy timber between. Behind me stands Devil's Peak and the seven lakes for which this basin is named.

I sit on the bluff and enjoy a peace so perfect, I let out a moan. The wind caressing my face feels and smells like the breath of God, sweet and warm, offering an opportunity for intimacy not often found amidst the noise and clamor of city streets. It's as if I'm sitting in the arms of Creator, sheltered beneath eagle's wings. It's easy to imagine those wings carrying me across the bluff, above the treetops and through the clouds until we touch the birthplace of the sun.

This is the way I always feel when I'm in the wilderness—the spiritual and physical worlds meld into one. I bask in the rightness until the sun stands still overhead, then I crawl up the bluff and around the shimmering jewel of Lake Ivern.

When I reach camp, I move my cot inside the canvas tent where I read a magazine published by a famous talk show host and wonder if she will invite my wild women to appear on her show. Tresa brought the magazine; it was her idea for us to appear on her show in the first place. I can imagine the lot of us showing up with an assortment of adventurous gear. Christy will wear her motorcycle leathers, Ada will be decked out in Peruvian Alpaca, and Sharon will top off her jeans and Ryder boots with a cowboy hat and checkered scarf. Jen will wear tennis shoes; Julie, a flannel shirt; and I'll wear camouflage with a pistol on my hip, although it will probably have to be unloaded for the show. And Tresa . . . well, Tresa will find something quite shocking to wear, of that I am sure . . . and worse . . . she'll have to do something shocking on the show. Just thinking about it gets me nervous.

At the moment, Tresa is off on an adventure of her own. I don't expect to see her until nightfall. She's an avid hiker, and on our first day out here I introduced her to off-trail exploration. After a trip to Boston Bluff, where we could view most of the Sky Lakes Wilderness, I gave her a map and compass and sent her off on her own. Now she's like a kid on Christmas morning.

Each evening we gather around a pine-scented campfire to share our adventures. I've stuck close to camp, so my adventures are more spiritual than physical. Creator seems so very close; I want to hold this feeling and take it back with me to civilization. Life takes on a kind of simplicity out here where the air carries the aroma of ponderosa pine and incense cedar.

While thinking these thoughts, a crash of thunder peels me off my cot. I pick myself up, push back the tent flap, and peer out.

Gray fog has dropped to the earth. Hard rain pelts my face. Such an abrupt change of weather is not rare, but it can be dangerous in the wilderness. I scurry into the tent and grab my coat and hat. Then I head out to brave the rain and take stock of the situation.

Blustery wind stings my eyes, and I can feel the hair on my arms standing straight up. That gets my blood roiling. Cat has told me more than once about this strange phenomenon just before lighting strikes.

I hurry across the clearing and run into the forest just seconds before a finger of lightning skitters through the black sky. It barely misses the dead snag leaning at a precarious angle over the tent.

Five days ago Tresa climbed that dead snag to hang a US flag. Transfixed, I stare at the flag, as its red and white stripes whip angrily in the wind. It's as if the flag is shaking a fist in the face of God.

Suddenly, I want to be as far away from it as I can be.

An immediate roar follows the next flash of lightning. I don't even have time to begin the slow count of seven to guess the distance. There *is* no distance. I am in the center of the storm. I run from the trees and turn circles in a small clearing.

Which tree will the lightning strike next?

My fear of lightning began back when I was seven years old on our little ranch in Fort Jones. I overheard my parents talking about how lightning plowed through the bedroom window of a farmer and his wife and whacked them both dead with one strike. It struck another farmer while he was sitting on his tractor. Later, when I worked as a Dean's assistant at Old Dominion University in Virginia, my fear was sealed. Lightning was striking people dead on a regular basis, but it hit too close to home when it struck down Governor Godwin's son on an exposed beach ... the same beach I frequented.

Now, I feel too exposed in the open meadow. Another crash of thunder and a flood of water dumps from the sky, soaking me and making quick rivulets in the hard earth. The air carries the smell of wet grass and mud. The sky is black and swirling. Echoes of thunder reverberate and my skin prickles at the cold. I think about hypothermia and wonder how far Tresa has wandered from camp. We're miles from the trailhead.

Suddenly I catch a flash of iridescent green flapping in the wind. It's Tresa's rain poncho. She's flying across the log that serves as a bridge over the nearby creek. She looks more like a wild animal than a woman, hidden as she is beneath the folds of her enormous poncho.

"We're in for a storm!" she hollers. I can barely hear her over the rush of wind and clashing thunder. Her eyes burn with the fire of excitement. "This is just great! Let's head to the bluff."

"You're nuts!" I shout, but she can't hear me. She's twirling in the wind, her upturned face shining with wetness. When the next bolt of lightning flashes across the meadow, Tresa doesn't even flinch. "We can see everything from there," she says.

"Yeah, right," I mumble. "If we're not turned into crispy critters."

But I grab my rifle and lead the way, hoping Tresa won't smell the fear that clinches my heart. It's a strange kind of fear, more like two parts anticipation, one part terror. We climb the draw overlooking Lake Ivern. It's tucked into a small, hidden crater with no inlet or outlet. On the far side of the lake, a narrow spit of land separates the shore from a 300-foot drop that borders Boston Bluff. Few people come here because it's far from the other six lakes, at the end of the trail.

"We're not going out!" I yell over the pounding rain. "We'll get close as we can without committing suicide."

Tresa gives me a slow nod, her reluctant sign of agreement. I turn back to the bluff, grateful for the thickness of the forest canopy that partially protects us. Howling wind shatters the forest sending loose branches that we call "widow makers" crashing to the ground. Towering pines spin madly and throw rain-soaked cones in every direction. I stand near a giant cedar. Its red-planked bark acts as a shield between the errant missiles and me. My cowboy hat also offers a bit of protection should anything fall straight down. I sling my rifle over my shoulder and fold my arms across my chest hoping to appear calm, perhaps even a bit bored.

Tresa is still staring at me, so I swallow and buck up my shoulders. It's about time for a little excitement in my life. I can't believe I was sitting in the tent reading not more than fifteen minutes ago. Where's the wild in that?

Everything smells of wet earth as we slide down the steep cavern to the last row of giant firs near the shore of Lake Ivern. From here, we have a clear view of the sheer face of Boston Bluff. A massive spray of white fog has dropped out of the main bank of clouds. It whirls around the bluff, creating a shimmering mass of translucent light amidst the storm.

The change is astounding. Was it just this morning that I viewed the bluff as my sanctuary, a place where I met Creator? Tresa and I stare as the cloud changes shapes and colors. The cloud seems like a live thing, a being from another dimension making its presence known. I feel as if I stare at it hard and long enough I may just see the face of God.

I glance at Tresa wanting to say something, wondering if she feels the same way I do . . . that we are about to touch the metaphysical, but the wind is too noisy to do any kind of talking. I am no longer frightened. The storm has become a light show, complete with sound effects, better than fireworks on the Fourth of July, and we have front row seats.

Tresa must feel the same way, because she nods and smiles at me, and then we turn back to watch the scene.

The cloud keeps changing shapes, transforming into an angel of pulsating colored light. The storm-blackened demon of a sky forms a backdrop that makes the light appear even brighter. It nearly blinds us with its brilliance. Thunder and the sound of rushing wind add an eerie effect, as if the cloud is an enormous living creature. It glistens and throbs, vibrating with unreleased power.

If I ever doubted the existence of a Creator, I don't now. Something totally Other created this spellbinding display.

The cloud hovers over the bluff, swirling like a whirlpool, forcing all its energy into a restrained blob. The blob trembles and quivers until the shuddering mass of energy tumbles from the bluff. It plows straight for us in a powerful force of howling wind.

We brace ourselves for the expected pummeling.

I think of the time a hurricane took out an entire row of houses within a mile of my small apartment in Virginia. I wonder if this wind will carry Tresa and me away, but there is no fear in my wondering. Part of me yearns to be caught up in the cloud. I'm intoxicated with wonder.

The cloud hits us with one long swoosh.

Tresa and I cling to nearby trees to keep from being carried away. The boom of a thousand cannons deafens us. Hail begins to pound the ground. The forest canopy shelters us from the worst of the pummeling. Enormous drops of hail bounce straight up from the lake. Geysers form across the surface until it looks as if the lake is a foot higher than the bank. The hail-filled cloud charges like a freight train across the water and over the mountain. The roar of it is strong in our ears.

Then, it is gone.

An awesome stillness follows the hail. The sky is still dark, but all wind has stopped. Lake Ivern lies still and placid, glimmering like an iridescent haven. Not even the twitter of a bird breaks the eerie silence while the forest waits in anticipation.

Tresa and I remain transfixed, our eyes riveted on the bluff. I realize I've been holding my breath while staring at a single gnarled tree that stands bravely on the rock.

Suddenly, a forked strike of lightning reaches out of the clouds and blasts the far point of the bluff next to the tree—the exact point where we usually stand.

"Yes!" Tresa and I cry out together, each throwing a fist into the air.

Thoughts of Elijah and the whirlwind fill my mind—Moses talking to the burning bush. The shepherd boy, David, writing of God parting the heavens and coming down with dark clouds under his feet. God, himself, talking in the book of Job, *"Can you raise your voice to the clouds and cover yourself with a flood of water? Do you send the lightning bolts on their way? Do they report to you, 'Here we are'?"*

I envision a laughing Creator, raising his voice to the clouds and covering himself with torrents of rain—a Creator very much in touch with His creation—a Creator who is also Redeemer.

Tresa and I dance our way out to the upper bluff and stand in full view of Devil's Peak. A swirling, angry, red sky rises above it, but we are invincible, tucked away as we are in the palm of God's hand. Our laughter echoes off the bluff, tumbling into the crevice below. The feeling of invincibility stays with us until all light falls from the heavens and we have no choice but to creep through the dark making our way back to camp.

3

Enemy Who Strikes Fear

Through the Jungle very softly
flits a shadow and a sigh—
He is Fear, O Little Hunter, he is Fear!

—*Rudyard Kipling*

**October 2009, Still between Wednesday and Thursday
Dad's hospital room**

While sitting in the hospital chapel, a pang of anxiety
hits me full in the chest. I jump to my feet and run back
down the stairs to Dad's room. I pull up a chair next to his
bed and hold his hand, expecting him to be alert. His eyes
are open looking straight at me, but when I squeeze his
hand there's no response.

Disappointment slows my heartbeat. I'm not sure
what I expected, but it certainly wasn't this. Dad is exactly
the same as when I left him. I wonder if he wishes I would
leave him and go home. He said as much on his second
night here before the tube was stuck down his throat.

"Go home!" he demanded, but then he broke into a
coughing fit, and I was glad to be there to hand him needed
tissues and water. The nurse had already said she was
overworked and would appreciate the help, so I sat up all
night in the hard window seat, avoiding the comfortable

chair, in order to give Dad his privacy while remaining close enough to meet his needs.

Now, I wonder if he would tell me to go home, if he could talk, or if he is afraid to be alone.

I nearly laugh at the thought. My dad? The Marine? Afraid? Ha! Like that would ever happen. Fear is not a word I would ever use to describe Dad.

When I was ten years old Dad took me on a road trip from Fort Jones to Weed. Back in those days it took a few hours to crawl north up the winding two-lane highway over the pass to Yreka and then fight the traffic back south along the river road toward the small town of Weed. Fighting traffic was one of Dad's biggest challenges. More than a few times he elicited screams from my mother's throat and sent me crawling onto the back floorboard when he pulled out of a line of twenty or so cars and tried to pass them all. This, while an oncoming, honking car was heading straight at us!

Some patient, courteous driver would always put their foot on the brake and let Dad back in line (helping him live up to his nickname, Lucky), but not before Momma and I imagined ourselves either plummeting headlong over the sheer drop of the mountain or plowing into the oncoming car. It never did much good for Dad to pass all those cars, because Momma would end up in tears and I ended up nauseous.

"Gonna throw up," I would moan.

"It's all in your head, Sandra," Dad always said.

I held my sickness as long as I could, but never long enough. Motion sickness has always been a problem of mine.

So, when Dad decided to take me with him on the trip to Weed, he also decided to skip all those curvy roads and piled up traffic. Instead, he drove straight east, right across the meadows and through the forest and over the mountains. Momma stayed at home, while we traveled no road at all!

I remember hanging onto the doorjamb while our pickup bounced all over the place. A time or two, it leaned so heavily that I thought it would turn over and keep right on rolling into the creek bed several hundred feet below. When we finally made it down to the flatlands and could see the town of Weed off in the distance, I was proud of myself for having never once cried out or making Dad stop so I could throw up my breakfast.

Dad was proud of me too.

These days, when I point out the path we took to my friends, they never believe me. Even as an adult those mountains look monstrous. And to think we drove right over the top!

There's no doubt about it ... my sense of wild adventure came straight from my father.

Now, sitting with Dad, I chuckle at the memory and feel a slight squeeze from his hand. When I look up he's staring back at me, so I remind him of our adventure. A smile crosses his face. Though I cannot see his mouth through all the medical equipment, I see the lines around his eyes crinkle.

"Those were good times, weren't they Dad? And remember all our fishing trips?"

Even while asking, I have to suppress a moan. I remember too many fishing trips when we spent more time trying to repair an engine or recover lost equipment than we did fishing, and one particular nightmare of a trip when Dad dropped a boat engine into the lake. We fished for that engine the entire night.

Truth is I never did like fishing. I never caught a thing, unless you count submerged bushes and logs, and I could never stomach putting a worm on a hook. But I never fessed up because of two things. First, I never wanted to miss an adventure and second, those fishing trips always gave Dad plenty of time to talk with me.

Another irony. When I was growing up, Dad talked and I listened. "Children are to be seen, and not heard," Dad often said, and I took it to heart. Few people could get a word out of me. These days I tease my husband that I'm making up for lost time.

Here with Dad, that's certainly true. I'm doing all the talking while he can only listen.

"Fishing trips and Look candy bars are what I remember," I say to Dad. We always stopped for a candy bar on the way home. Momma tried to keep us in line with healthy food but both Dad and I craved sweets.

Suddenly Dad looks anxious and I wonder if he's okay.

I wave at the nurse sitting at the hall monitor on the other side of the glass. She's been watching us the entire time. She comes in to take Dad's pulse. "Are you afraid?" She says to Dad.

My mouth is open, ready to tell her that Dad is *never* afraid, but before I can get a word out, Dad nods his head. My throat closes as if someone is choking me. To make matters worse, there is no mistaking the fear in his eyes.

I'm too nonplussed to hear the words of comfort the nurse speaks to Dad. She's one of my favorites, and I know she believes in God. I remain mute while she lays a hand on his shoulder and speaks softly, but when she returns to her station I follow.

"I don't understand," I say.

She turns sympathetic blue eyes toward me.

"This often happens at this stage," she says.

"But . . ." I stammer, "Dad's a believer. He's even seen Heaven and told me he's ready to go."

I'm thinking of the fact that at the age of 50 a massive heart attack propelled Dad into an out-of-body experience where he saw God. Dad didn't want to return to this earth, but he did, and for over 30 years he never once forgot the power of that metaphysical experience. So why aren't those memories working for him now?

When I ask the nurse, she nods. "We also have a real enemy who likes to hit us at our weakest," she says. She goes on to explain how the drugs and pain play a part, as well as the long hours through the night with little sleep. "Just keep praying for him," she says. "This feeling of fear always passes for believers."

Maybe for Dad, I think, but what about me? I'm totally shaken that my father is afraid. I've never before in my entire life seen him afraid of anything.

4

Safe Places

Weak and wounded sinner
Lost and left to die
O, raise your head, for love is passing by

—Chris Rice

**October 2009, Still between Wednesday and Thursday
Dad's hospital room**

Back in Dad's room, the nurse turns on a light
and injects more pain killer into the intravenous tube
connected to his arm. Then she leans over and comforts
him with words of God's love. I marvel at her compassion
and sensitivity. She has shared several shifts with me and
is well aware that both Dad and I worship the Living God
of the Bible. I speak of God a little differently than she
does (I call him Creator Redeemer), but both of us believe
in the truth of his written word.

While she performs various nursing tasks I read
through some of the most comforting phrases ever written.

From Psalm 48, verse 14, I read, "For this God is our
God for ever and ever; he will be our guide even to the
end."

I continue reading through Psalm 49 and stop at verse
15, making sure I capture Dad's eyes before repeating it.
Dad is looking at me intently while I read, "But God will

redeem my soul from the grave; he will surely take me to himself."

Dad is calm now, and his eyes are closing. He will soon be asleep. I kiss him on the forehead, one of the few places on his body without some kind of medical contraption sticking out of it. Then I plop back on the chair and read Psalm 46, but I don't need to look at the words on the paper. I know this one by heart.

"God is our refuge and strength, an ever present help in trouble."

I pause to emphasize each word of the next phrase. "THEREFORE . . . WE WILL NOT FEAR. Though the earth gives way and the mountains fall into the heart of the sea."

I repeat it again, more for myself than for Dad. His eyes are shut and his breathing is steady. I continue reading the Psalm, nourishing sweet comfort for myself. Before I close my Bible, I read two notes I've written in the margins. One says, "Creator Redeemer dwells in me. Anywhere Creator Redeemer dwells is a safe place."

I choke on the last phrase. Everyone who enters and leaves this unit squirts their hands with sanitizer found on little shelves next to every doorway and elevator. Most of the healthy people passing through the Critical Care Unit also wear face masks to protect themselves from the billions of germs floating in the air. Swine Flu has recently claimed dozens of victims in the Rogue Valley, and this ward houses many of them. Dad has already fought several viruses that have attacked his body since being in this place. The doctor tells me Dad will probably have to fight even more before he leaves.

This is *not* a safe place.

Yet volunteers, nurses and doctors march through here every day to help heal the wounded and sick.

Anywhere Creator Redeemer dwells is a safe place.

I think about that for a long time, coming to the conclusion that safety isn't always about freedom from pain, worry, stress, or even fear. Safety is a matter of place, yet it is also a matter of attitude. It is possible that I can be safe and not know it.

That thought gets my mind spinning, so I read the other note in my margin. It says simply, "Creator Redeemer knows what he's doing."

It is a good reminder, because I believe Creator Redeemer only has good in mind for those who have claimed His gift. Yet I cannot help but wonder what possible good can come out of my Dad having to suffer such agony.

I close my Bible and lean back against the chair. The first day Dad was in the hospital he told me God was taking him home. I had argued with him then, not wanting to believe it. Even though he only has two thirds of his heart following his heart attack years ago, Dad is a healthy man. He still maintains a full truck garden and performs all kinds of work around the house. Few of us younger people can keep up with him when he gets moving in any one direction.

Yet even while arguing with Dad, I felt a quaking in my heart and *knew* his words were true. Then just as quickly, I had denied it. But all the denying in the world won't change the truth.

"You know I'm ready to go?" Dad had asked

"Sure," I answered. "I know, but don't be silly. We're not ready for you to go."

Clay, my youngest son was in the room at the time and, even though he loves his grandpa with all his heart, he agreed. "You're going to a much better place," he told Dad.

Two days later, when Dad looked well enough to return home and after the doctor had given him a good report, I took a short break to run to the post office. When I returned to the hospital, it seemed as if every doctor in the place was in Dad's room. A team of technicians and medical students hovered in the hall trying to get a glimpse inside. Momma was already there.

I pushed through the crowd. "What's going on?"

Anxious eyes looked at me, but no one ventured an answer. Momma hovered on one side of Dad and a doctor on the other. They had moved him from his bed to a gurney.

"What about a breathing tube?" the doctor asked Dad.

Dad shook his head. "No."

"Hank," Momma said. "You have to do this."

Dad shook his head again, "No."

The doctor looked at me. I stood there with my mouth open for several heartbeats until I finally realized the doctor was asking me to support my father.

"Are you sure about this?" I asked Dad.

"Yes." His reply was weak but firm. I searched his eyes for any signs of wavering. They were perfectly clear. Honestly, he looked as if he could get up out of that bed and walk away. I wanted to grab him and do that very thing, but the doctors were already wheeling the gurney down the hallway. I nearly had to run to keep up.

Momma was running too, but both of us stopped when we reached the service elevator.

"You have to take the other elevator," the doctor said. "There's a waiting room outside the Critical Care Unit."

Momma had already punched the down button. Neither of us said a word while the elevator groaned its way to the next floor. When the doors opened, we sprinted down the hall. At least a dozen white-coated personnel had congregated around Dad's gurney. Momma was right behind them as they pushed through the metal doors that separated the Critical Care Unit from the rest of the hospital.

One nurse held up her hand and hollered, "Stop!"

I did as I was told.

Momma kept going.

Several hospital workers surrounded Momma and kept saying that she had to leave, promising to come get her after Dad was settled.

"That's my husband!" Momma hollered, "I'm NOT leaving him."

I was prouder of my mother at that moment than I had ever been in my life. I took a step toward her but then stopped. She would have a better chance of staying if at least one of us did what we were told. I backed up and the doors slammed shut.

Thinking of the incident now, while looking at the unwanted tube stuck down Dad's throat, I wonder if things would have been different if I had stayed with Momma. And if things had turned out differently would that be a good thing? Would Dad already be gone? How would I feel about that?

Does God really know what he's doing?

I notice the slip in my thinking. The term "God" for me is out there, impersonal, perhaps caring, perhaps not, a rule maker.

On the other hand, Creator Redeemer touches the hidden places of my heart. Creator knows all about me, because he formed me. I know Psalm 139 by heart; have even set it to music. It claims that Creator knew me before the world began; he called me by name; he saw me while I was yet in my mother's womb. However, if he is only Creator then there is still the question of how much he is involved with my life and whether he is still the rule maker ready to whack me when I mess up.

I remind myself that God is not only Creator, but he is also Redeemer.

Redeemer is the one who gave his life in my place, who paid the penalty for all my mess ups, who is closer than a friend, and who knows every word before it is on my tongue. If Creator Redeemer knows what he's doing, and I believe he does, then *all* things work for good . . . even the tube running down my father's throat.

The realization gives me a bit of comfort and a large amount of hope. I turn off the light and move to the window seat.

Dad looks as if he will be asleep for a while. The nurse must have given him a sleeping pill. He's usually awake more often at night than during the day, which means I should be taking advantage of this time to sleep but, though my body is tired, my mind is wide awake. I've been awake for nearly 36 hours and only managed a few minutes at a time before that. Nurses and technicians pop in here at least once an hour. They try to be quiet, but I always wake up. I'm on alert the same as with each of my five children when they were babies. I slept light then, too, listening for every murmur.

Now I hear only the steady in and out swoosh of the respirator. Grabbing a metal rod, I pull open the window blinds and stare at the moonlight breaking through a clouded sky. As I watch the moon dance I wonder if there was ever another time when Dad was afraid and I had simply overlooked it.

The first thing that comes to mind is when I was four years old. Mom and Dad were sitting in the front seat of our car while I rode in the back. We were traveling south down the winding road below Prospect, Oregon. For whatever reason, I unlocked the door and opened it. Dad heard the sound of rushing wind and looked back to see my small body spinning through the air.

"I thought you were dead, Sandra," he told me later. "You were in that ditch, covered with blood and buried in leaves, but when I bent down to pick you up, you smiled at me."

I have no doubt Dad felt fear at that moment, and all the moments following while he raced me to the doctor's office in Shady Cove. Momma held me on her lap and kept asking me if I was all right, but I just kept saying, "Shut up, Momma. Shut up, Momma." She insists I was a difficult child even back then.

I ended up with a concussion, which is probably the reason for my motion sickness and periodic double vision, but other than that I was fine after an overnight stay in a Medford hospital.

Another time I know Dad felt fear was when he was sixteen years old and stationed on a Coast Guard ship during World War II. Dad told me the story many times.

"A kamikaze pilot was coming straight for us," Dad said. "My hands froze on the gun wheel, and I was unable to push the button to fire. It took three men to pry my fingers off. They shot the plane out of the sky just before it hit us."

I was nearly sixteen when Dad told me the story, the same age as Dad when he went through the experience. It made me shudder to imagine having to go to war. Dad didn't fess up till much later about how he was able to get into the service at such a young age. Both, my Dad and his cousin Henry, shared the same first and last names, but Henry was two years older. Dad used Henry's birth certificate to sign up for the war.

There are many times when Dad should have been afraid in his childhood—like the time when he was bitten by a cottonmouth and his healer grandmother laid a raw steak on the wound to draw out the poison. She gathered herbs to keep him alive while he was in and out of consciousness for a couple of days.

Then there was the time Dad climbed into his father's beehives and was stung over every inch of his young body. Or maybe the time when his horse turned left and he kept going straight over the top and his head connected with a log. He was also afraid as a youngster when his father, Deputy US Marshall John Speed Taylor, took him by horseback to transport prisoners across state lines. I'll never forget Dad's stories about sleeping around the campfire and wondering what would happen if any of those prisoners broke their bonds.

Dad wasn't afraid of tornadoes until one came through the nearby town of Salina, Oklahoma, and destroyed everything in its path. Dad lived at Atilee at the time, high in the foothills of the Ozarks and, as a lawman, Grandpa Taylor had to travel to town to check things out. He told Dad to stay home on the farm where he belonged. Dad was old enough to think he knew best, and young enough not to think of the possibilities. He only saw the opportunity to find free money.

"There was money all over the place," Dad told me. "I thought I had hit the jackpot, until I noticed body parts and dead people. Couldn't get out of there fast enough, and I haven't liked tornadoes ever since."

Thinking of the story now, I wouldn't categorize Dad's feelings regarding tornados as fear. At least it isn't the kind of fear that immobilizes a person. He would rather not face a tornado if given a choice, but if the meeting is inevitable, he will face it with courage. Lots of things in life are like that.

For instance, right now I would rather not face this hospital. I would much rather be in the wilderness where the wind carries the breath of Creator Redeemer. Yet, like with all the hard things in life, I'm determined to keep mustering the courage to do what must be done. Yes. Fear is involved. I'm afraid of losing my father ... and I'm also afraid for my mother. In the past sixty years, she's never known a time without Dad being there for her. How on earth can she face a future without him?

A shudder ripples across my shoulders as I turn from the window. Fear seems to be a necessary ingredient in life; in the very least it's a given. Each of us *will* experience fear sometime throughout our lives. It's what we do with it that makes the difference. Fear will either lead us to Creator Redeemer, or it will lead us away from him.

Lifting my eyes back to the clouded sky, I whisper a prayer to Creator Redeemer, admitting I am afraid of many things, the biggest being that I will not be the encouragement my father needs of me in these late hours. Yet, even as I admit my fear, I know I have been a help to my father this night. He is sleeping peacefully now after my endless reading of scripture.

I unfold a blanket and lie down, my thoughts drifting toward Cat. I wonder how he's holding up, having to act as both guide and cook. Cooking over a fire is time-consuming, not just in cook time, but also in cutting and gathering of wood for fuel. I think about the lovely smell of incense cedar and ponderosa pine that fills the air at base camp. I pretend I'm there now, beneath the canvas tent with Cat, and my mind travels back to where our wilderness adventures began.

Part Two
Strange Ideas

I see a mountain with blue skies above,
Streams flowing, birds singing.
I see a valley with hot city streets,
And people rushing everywhere
Give me the mountain and I will be free.
Give me the valley, I'll tell others of you.
I'd take the mountain, Lord,
For the feeling I would feel,
But the valley is where I will be.

—*Sandy Cathcart*

5

Reconnecting

> Once in everyone's life
> there is apt to be a period when he is fully awake,
> instead of half asleep.
> —*E.B. White*

Spring, 1986
Applegate Valley, Southern Oregon

I'm at a friend's house, sitting in a circle of women who are sharing their stories about the perfect anniversary.

"What's the perfect setting?" Nancy asks.

"Paradise," Jennifer answers. "Cute little cottages, my husband wearing a tuxedo and me beautiful in a fancy dress, candlelight dinner in the lodge, and my husband rowing me beneath the moonlight on the pond."

"Ummmm."

I try to imagine Cat in a tuxedo but can't quite manage it. He might consent for a friend's wedding . . . a really close friend . . . or perhaps for a funeral. I shake my head. Probably not. Certainly not for a dinner. I look around the room.

My friends are getting serious now, chattering and exchanging ideas. No one seems to notice I have nothing to offer. I'm thinking it would be fun to dress up and go somewhere special like that, and I feel the first little wisps of resentment floating around my head. Why can't Cat dress in a tuxedo for me? Aren't I worth it?

Ugh. I know these thoughts will lead to a bad end, so I force myself to turn them in a different direction. After all, isn't an anniversary for both man and wife? So what would be the perfect anniversary setting for Cat?

I laugh.

The room goes suddenly quiet; all those heavily made up eyes turn in my direction.

"What?" I say.

Jennifer knows me, and she has a twinkle in her eye. "What are you laughing about?" she asks.

"I was just thinking that anniversaries are for both parties, so what would be the perfect setting for the man?"

Jennifer chuckles and Nancy's mouth drops open, then she shakes her head and says, "Somewhere in the outdoors, that's for sure."

All the women laugh and return to their chatter.

While they negotiate fancy dinners, I make plans of my own ... Cat and me on a motorcycle, flying down the road ... a winding road ... to? The beach. Cat likes the beach. We'll sleep in a pup tent protected by a sand dune. We'll eat dinner over an open fire. He'll love it.

And he did.

During the first part of our trip I figured I had lost my mind to have suggested a long-distance motorcycle trip. It was no cruiser with a cushy winged-backed seat we were riding, but a Yamaha Virago, a trimmed-down sport bike. Cat took the curves at the speed of light. I clung to his middle, forcing myself to lean with him while my mind screamed to pull the other way, especially when we leaned so far that the foot pedals created sparks on the pavement. More than once, I envisioned the two of us flying into the air and sliding across the highway until every bit of our skin was scraped off. It was not a pretty picture.

"Relax," Cat yelled over the roaring engine.

Yeah right. No matter how hard I tried to force myself into relaxing, it just wouldn't happen, so I prayed, asking God to please keep us alive.

Your life is in my hands.

It was a whisper from Creator Redeemer, and my heart immediately recognized it as truth. If this day should end up being the day for me to die, then what better way than by doing something passionate with the person I loved most in the whole world? As Cat took the next corner, I relaxed and felt the oneness of our bodies melding into a single unit, becoming part of a rhythm as old as the earth. We leaned far to the right, then swung back up and leaned left. Up down, up around, like a river flowing timelessly inside its banks. By the time we reached the Oregon coast I was so relaxed I was falling asleep.

Cat was driving with one hand now, while his other hand held both of mine at his waist to keep me from falling off. Finally, he pulled into a rest stop at Humbug Mountain. He parked the bike and both of us climbed off, barely making it to the grass before we fell to the ground. We woke an hour later, discovering we were less than a foot off the main path. Other travelers were making a wide berth around us, staring as if we had dropped in from another planet. Cat and I burst out in unified laughter, then he pulled me to my feet and we climbed back on the bike.

The rhythm came easy now, even though a strong wind whipped across the beach hitting us full in the face. The roar of it filled our ears, so we couldn't even talk with one another. I imagined the hard wind whipping sand into my eyes and hair when we would set up camp for the night, but Cat met me with a surprise of his own. He booked a motel room overlooking the sea. In the end, we both agreed it was a perfect anniversary.

The following year we set aside a week and rode up the coast to the Washington Peninsula where we pulled onto a ferry and headed to Canada. Because we rode a motorcycle we were the first on and off the ferry. Everyone talked with us as if they knew us.

"You're the folks riding the motorcycle?"

"Yeah."

Then they would proceed to tell us all the fun places to go and see, the secret places that only the locals knew about.

It was like the difference between seeing a television documentary about an adventure or actually taking part in the adventure. When we passed a farm, we smelled the musky scent of cows and manure. When it rained, we felt hard drops pelting our arms and soaking our jeans. When the sun beat down on us, we looked for shade from a moving truck to provide a bit of relief.

That motorcycle trip became a yearly thing for us. We began taking two and three-week trips traveling as far as Wyoming and Montana. On one trip a three-point buck challenged us over four lanes of open highway. We laughed at how he ducked his head and turned around as if we were another buck after his harem.

In return for my willingness to do some of the things Cat enjoyed, he started doing some things with me, like watching a movie or attending the local historical meetings. One night, we flung open the living room windows, turned off the lights and leaned into each other's arms as we listened to the booming chords of Rachmaninoff. I think every one of my fancy girlfriends would have considered that night as romantic as anything they could have dreamed up.

My ultimate challenge was to enter Cat's hunting world. For years he had been asking me to join him, but I didn't understand the concept of killing an animal, though admittedly, I was a hypocrite. I loved the taste of elk meat as long as someone else did the killing, but I couldn't imagine aiming a rifle at that beautiful animal. Yet, after years of Cat returning home from his hunting trips and talking about the beauty of the animals and how much he enjoyed being out in the woods with them, I finally realized Cat cared for those animals as much as I did.

Then one day, I followed a herd for over three hours.

While still in my nightgown, I spotted about 20 elk spreading through the forest. Without changing clothes, I pulled on a pair of slippers and sneaked out my back door, moving into the forest when the animals weren't looking. One young bull passed so close to me I could have stretched out my arm and touched him. He must have outweighed me by at least a hundred pounds, and the top of his back was above my head. I slowed my heart and held my breath, hoping he wouldn't think I was any kind of threat.

When the 20 moved on, I saw 25 more behind me. Their musky scent overpowered the smell of spicy Manzanita and wet earth. My ears tuned in to their simple noises—a gentle mew, the snap of their bending knees, the clunk of overturning rocks.

When the herd moved up the hill, I followed. A couple of times they saw me moving and took off at a run. I ran after them, thinking I had lost the herd, but then I would bend down and spot their golden rumps standing perfectly still. My gaze would follow the curve of their backs up to their deep brown eyes staring straight at me. We played this game several times until they accepted me as one of their own, and all of us spread across a high mountain meadow in perfect peace.

When I returned home, I dialed Rocky Mountain Elk Foundation. Dan Crockett, the director of publications, answered the phone. After telling him about my experience, he asked me to write an article about it. I accepted the challenge, and ended my story by saying it was the first time I thought I might be able to hunt.

Dan called me back. "I want you to finish the story," he said. "Go out and hunt and tell us what it's like."

My voice shook a little as I agreed to the assignment.

Cat returned home the next day with a rifle for me. He smiled as I fitted the smooth wood into my hands. Until that moment I hadn't realized how much he had wanted me to be a part of his passion. Target practice became a weekly outing and, for a year, I prepared for the hunt, not knowing if I could really shoot an animal, yet believing I could do anything if Cat was there with me. But then an opportunity arrived just days before hunting season—a local outfitter asked Cat to work as a guide.

"Uhhhh—" Cat hesitated.

"Of course, he'll do it," I said. It was one of Cat's biggest dreams to be able to work doing something he loved in the outdoors.

Cat looked at me. "But—"

"It's okay," I assured him. "I'll hunt solo and tell you all about it."

I kept a smile on my face but my heart was melting. How could I hunt alone?

Cat trained me well, but I was praying hard for someone to take pity on me. A week before opening day four male friends, Gary Shaw, Mike Calderwood, Cam Sturm, and Bruce Brown—all seasoned hunters—offered to take me with them. "Yes," I said, a little too quickly. "I would love that."

I slept at home, rose at three in the morning, and made the trek to my partners' campsite each morning. I never bagged a bull, didn't shoot at anything living or nonliving, but I learned a lot about how to track animals and the importance of camaraderie among hunters. The experience helped prepare me for the next year when Cat's hunting boss called me at the last minute saying his cook had canceled.

"I've never prepared meals for a bunch of hunters," I protested.

"No different than cooking for anyone else," Ron said. "Cat tells me you have plenty experience cooking over an open fire."

"Yeah, but—"

"He also says you still cook for an army even though your five children are grown."

"Yeah, but—"

"I'll have everything ready for you."

But that was not the case, and the first day about did me in. Cat dropped me off in base camp but had to scurry off to help Ron tidy up after a horse wreck at one of the trailheads. I sat shivering in a cold, dark camp trailer while the burly hunters gathered around a campfire outside. I had already hauled several buckets of water from the creek, boiled the water so it could cool for drinking, and rummaged through Ron's meager stash of supplies trying to figure out what to fix for dinner. I ended up throwing hamburgers at the hungry hunters. This was the first of ten days I had committed to and exhaustion had already taken hold of me. I groaned as I hovered in the little trailer and prayed for strength. I was already sick of the trip. Then I heard the guys talking outside.

"I saved up 364 days for this trip," André said.

"Yep," answered Doug. "It's bound to be a good one."

I laughed at the absurdity. André was looking at the next ten days as one of the best times of his life, while I viewed the same trip as a colossal disaster. I vowed at that moment to do all I could to change my attitude. I pulled out a sheet of paper and started making a list of supplies I would return home for the next day and, while I was there, I would bake a pie that would bring the men running back to camp.

My plan worked—in spite of a record snowfall, in spite of having to break ice off the creek to carry water, and in spite of the fact I forgot to bring flour for the gravy and tried using pancake mix instead. No one could eat the resulting concoction, so the men used my gravy to stick notes on the camp refrigerator.

I ended up enjoying the next ten days so much that I didn't want to return home. The men loved my cooking, shared their stories with me over the campfire, and listened intently when I related my own afternoon escapades hunting solo. It was the first of many years of sharing my husband's passion for hunting, and though I've carried my rifle and combed the woods, I've never once shot an animal. Turns out, that's the way it is for most hunters. I would have never dreamed that hunting has so little to do with killing and so much to do with relationship both, with the camaraderie of other hunters, and connection with the land and the One who created it.

October 2009, Between Wednesday and Thursday
Dad's hospital room

Thinking about that camaraderie now in the dark hours of the deep night, I remember that Dad, too, was a hunter who provided meat for our table during lean years when he had no other way to do so. I wish he could get out of bed now and come with me to Base Camp. It's one of the things I hoped to do with him someday. He would love it there sitting around the fire and telling hunting stories; the men would love him. The art of telling stories is highly valued in Elk Camp.

The thought makes me wonder if a silky bronze pine martin is darting from tree to tree in the quiet cool of the evening while Cat sleeps at Bessie Shelter. I can almost hear the singing creek and clunk of mule's feet. I imagine the soothing crackle of a warm fire and smell of warm leather as I finally fall into dreamland.

6

Empty Spaces

Love is found
In the things we've given up
More than in the things that we have kept.

—Rich Mullins

October 8, 2009
Dad's hospital room

All too soon, I awake to the sound of clinking glasses and loud chatter. The hands of the large clock on the wall register 7:00 a.m., the shift change. Rules state that visitors must leave the Critical Care Unit between the hours of seven and nine both morning and night. I manage to stay until after eight before I'm kicked out. I kiss Dad's forehead and let him know Momma will be here soon for the day shift. Then I head for the cafeteria.

After grabbing a plate of eggs and a muffin I find a table where I can look out the window and see Dad's room one floor above me. Momma has set up a signaling system where she will leave a box of facial tissues in the window if anything changes. Even though I know Momma's not there at the moment, I can't break the habit of sitting where I can see the signal.

The scrambled eggs are cold and tasteless, but I choke them down, knowing I need the brain fuel, especially in this time of high stress. I'm a brittle diabetic, which means I control my sanity with exercise, sleep, and several small meals throughout the day and evening.

I've had no exercise and little sleep, so I'm pretty sure my sanity could be in question. I'm usually the last person to know when I'm experiencing a low-glucose lack of intelligence. Cat is usually the first to inform me.

"You need to eat," he will say, and I always argue.

I always think it is an emotional issue, not a food one, until I finally put the food in my mouth and swallow it. The result is astounding. It's as if my eyes suddenly open, and I see the world in a different light.

Cat isn't here now to tell me if I'm doing okay, so I stuff the food in my mouth, one bite at a time and hope it is doing its magic. When I finish, I put away my tray and head back up to Dad's room.

I meet our youngest son, Clay, on the way. He visits every morning before work. This time he pulls me aside into the waiting room.

"Be nice to Grandma," he says.

I'm taken aback and my expression must show it, because he continues, "She's having a rough day."

I think I'm having a rough day too, and I wish my son would understand. "Of course," I say and mean it, but a part of me is also offended and hurt. *Aren't I always nice to my mother?*

Clay checks his watch. "Gotta run. Meeting with a client."

He gives me a quick hug and is gone. I suddenly feel empty and alone. Instead of returning to my father's hospital room, I plop into a nearby chair and try to recover some emotional strength. The waiting area is packed with people.

A young woman overdosed on drugs last night and an ambulance brought her into Critical Care. It seems as if half the people in the world claim to be her friends. They line the halls and fill the waiting room. I was either lucky getting this chair or someone must have seen my need without me realizing it. Looking at all the faces I wonder if the young woman has any idea how many people care for her, or perhaps, like me with my father, they waited too long to let her know.

My friend, Annie, took her life years ago.

When I received the news, my legs fell out from underneath me. If someone hadn't caught me and directed me to a chair, I would have fallen straight to the floor. All I could think was that I wasn't there when she needed me. She had asked me to visit many times, but I kept putting it off.

I was too busy, too far away, too short on motivation.

As I look at the young faces filling this room, I wonder how many of them feel the same way, and then I realize that's exactly how I've been with my parents—too busy, too far away, too short on motivation.

I've been nursing some anger at Momma for not calling me when Dad first showed signs of pneumonia. Perhaps he wouldn't be in here if I had seen how sick he was, but I can't honestly point that finger at Momma without pointing it right back at myself. If I had made it a habit to check on my parents more often, then I may have seen the danger myself and helped Dad avoid this place.

I say a silent prayer for the overdosed girl and her family, as well as for the friends filling this waiting room who may be feeling the same guilt I feel, and then I rise to return to my father's room.

I'm a bit afraid of facing Momma. When she and Dad are together it's like I don't even exist. Recently she's been referring to him as "her husband" even when talking with me. Just once, I wish she would say, "your father." Not long ago she and Dad filled a photo album of their lives together without one picture of me.

When I first saw that album, I felt as if I had been erased from their lives.

My brain knows better, even suspects Dad made that album for Momma to be able to remember him. Did he sense his time was short?

Dad's attending nurse is in the hallway, standing over the computer where she can see into the glass-walled room. It's a total fishbowl with no privacy at all, another necessary ingredient in trying to save a person's life. She nods at me as I enter the room.

Momma's standing over Dad, holding his hand. Her back is bent and she looks as frail as a baby bird after a failed flight. I feel bad for her, but I can't reach out and hug her, because we haven't shared that kind of relationship since I was a young girl. I'm not sure whatever came between us, but it is deeper and darker than the river that stands between Dad and me. It's a chasm without end, and I've never had the courage to ask her about it. I'm afraid I'll spiral into that chasm and never find my way out.

She leans over Dad and speaks the same words she's been saying every day since he's been here. "It's okay if you need to go," Momma says to Dad. "I'll be all right."

I know she means well. She's afraid he's hanging on and suffering because he's worried about her, but the words drive me crazy. I'm afraid if Dad hears them too often, he'll just give up the fight and leave us. I'm really not okay with that, but I keep the thought to myself.

I grab a chair and pull it to my side of Dad's bed. "Momma," I say, "here's a chair for you."

She ignores me and continues to talk to Dad. I figure she didn't hear me, so I bring the chair to her side and offer again. This time she tells me to keep the chair for myself.

"I've been sitting all night," I say.

She turns to me, and I see anger and what looks like hate written in the lines of her face. "Sandra!" she shouts. "I'm not an invalid. I don't need a chair."

I'm shocked at both the vehemence in her voice and the declaration. Does she really believe I think she's an invalid? This is the woman who was strong enough to withstand a team of medical personnel to stand by her husband. I see her as a strong woman, but I also see the frailty of someone in deep pain, a woman losing the only man she has ever loved. Everything in me wants to reach out to that pain, but I realize that now, as in every other instance in my life, I am not the one who can meet her needs.

Frustration slumps my shoulders as I carry the chair back to a corner and leave it sitting empty. I return to the other side of my father's bed and ask Momma why she is so mad at me.

She looks up and says in one breath, "I love you, Sandra, but I *don't* like you."

I swallow, remembering the rhyme we used to sing as children, *Sticks and stones may break my bones, but words can never hurt me.*

Boy, howdy, was that ever a lie. Momma's words slice through my heart as sharp as any sword. I tell myself she is distraught and doesn't really mean it. It's just her emotions looking for someone to blame. But then I remember that I can count on one hand the times she has visited me since my children have grown.

Momma is still looking at me, expecting a response, but I have none. At last she says, "And I think you feel the same way about me."

Out of the corner of my eye, I see Dad's expression change. His eyes widen and his mouth works as if he would like to say something. I cannot believe Momma and I are arguing right over the top of him, and him unable to say a word. I drop my voice to a whisper. "Momma, I don't have a heart of stone."

She turns back to Dad.

I stand there, like a deer caught in someone's headlights, until a flood of tears fills my eyes, then I turn and run sobbing down the hallway. Several nurses look at me, startled, but I keep moving right on through the double doors and into the hospital foyer. There are too many people in the waiting room so I keep on going until I'm outside where I walk back and forth in the rain and let my tears fall freely. Sobs still heave my chest up and down, but no one stops to question me or lend a shoulder.

My first thought is that Cat heard similar words from his mother when he was 18 years old and getting ready to fly overseas to fight a war in Vietnam. For the first time, I realize just how those words must have hurt him. My second thought is that Momma can't really mean it, but that thought doesn't last long. I know I've been a disappointment to her.

The third thought is whether or not she spoke the truth when she accused me of feeling the same way. I camp on that thought. Do I love my mother and not like her? Is that even possible?

I wrestle with the idea. Can a person truly love someone and not like them?

It just doesn't seem right. Yet, I've heard the phrase often enough and nearly always from someone who calls themselves a Christian, and certainly always from the person giving the love. But I wonder if they would be satisfied with that kind of love in return. Would they accept that kind of love from a spouse? Or from God?

Does God love me? But not like me?

Goodness! I feel like some kind of heretic just thinking the thought.

I find a stone bench partially sheltered from the pouring rain and I sit. I'm pretty sure if Cat were here at the moment, he would tell me to eat. I'm probably attempting to work from a glucose-starved brain, so I do the only thing I can do. I ask Creator Redeemer for help.

The result is immediate and clear.

Sanity enters my brain, and I realize that at this time, Momma cannot be held responsible for any words or actions. Her husband of over 60 years is fighting what is almost surely a losing battle for his life. In her entire life, she has never been alone. Whether her words to me are true or not makes little difference at this point. She needs someone to reach out to her.

Yet I cannot be the one to meet her needs. I, too, am in a stage of loss, losing the only father I have ever known.

I pull out my cell phone and call my Uncle Roy in Southern California. "You need to get here," I say. "Momma needs you."

It takes a bit of convincing. Like the rest of us, Roy still sees my father as strong and healthy and cannot believe this is truly a life-and-death battle, but he finally understands the urgency and promises to book a flight.

When I hang up, I feel both relieved and anxious. Roy is only four years older than me, the closest thing I've ever had to a brother, yet we are not close. Like Momma, he still remembers me for the things I did long ago, if he even thinks of me at all. When he arrives, it is quite possible I will feel all the more left out. But I know I've done the right thing.

So, why do I feel so empty?

Love is often found in the empty spaces.

It is Creator Redeemer's voice, but this time, while the rain pours around me, I'm struck by shame. The moment of sanity has passed. My glucose-starved brain is telling me I've given my mother plenty of reason to not like me. If I were her, I probably wouldn't like me either. In fact, I probably wouldn't love me.

And therein lies the problem. I don't believe my mother loves me, because I really don't believe you can love a person and not like them. So that leaves me with no love at all.

I'm a soaking mess, but my mind is processing the thought that Roy will be here for Momma and both of them will be here to care for Dad, so I am no longer needed.

I slip my cell phone back in my pocket and cross the parking lot to my car. Soon I am heading for the hills, back to the land I know and love. I'll pack my bags and be at the trailhead early in the morning. There's still time to ride into the wilderness and join Cat.

7

Defining Moments

Between the idea and the reality
Between the motion and the act
Falls the Shadow

—T.S. Eliot

October 8, 2009, Thursday
Lost Creek Lake, Southern Oregon

I always feel a sweet sense of freedom when my car reaches the top of Dam Hill. I'm not swearing, mind you; that's how all us locals refer to the steep grade leading to the top of the dam that holds back Lost Creek Lake. Wind has washed the sky clean of clouds here. When I cross the bridge on the far side of the lake, I pull off on an overlook and roll down the window, breathing in the fresh smell of moist earth and spicy Manzanita. My home is less than a mile away.

Guilt stabs my heart at having left everyone behind (meaning Dad and Momma and a ton of hospital staff), but it will be hours before they miss me. A part of my emotional makeup wants them to miss me, and yet another part wants to be free of that responsibility. I tell myself that my uncle will be here soon and Clay will transport my mother back and forth from the hospital to her home, so she can get rest at night.

I'm not really needed.

Yet even as I think the thought, I recall Momma's bent back and sad eyes.

I climb out of the car and let the wind slap my face. It blows over the mountain and down to the lake churning the water into white caps. The sound of crashing waves thunders up the shore.

A raven plops on the ground next to me. Though his feathers are ruffled he looks as if the wind is no problem at all. I click my tongue on the roof of my mouth and make a tock sound. The raven copies it. It's a trick Cat has taught me and I love doing it. I make two tocks, the raven makes two; I make one, the raven makes one. He's quite a copycat. When I tire of the game he gives a loud caw and whips away. I watch him hover and swoop, hover and swoop, until he finally disappears.

I wish I could disappear as easily as that raven.

It isn't the first time I've felt this way. A few defining moments in my childhood made me want to be an invisible girl. The first was an incident when I lived with my family on the ranch in Fort Jones. A distant relative showed up unexpectedly and followed me into the woods. My dog Nipper alerted me to trouble, and even though I had no idea what kind of trouble that might be, I trusted my dog's intuition enough to not answer when the man called out to me. When Nipper and I finally made our way back to the barn, Dad was there waiting. I'll never forget watching Dad using his strong fists to beat up that man when he came out of the woods. I learned much later that the man was a child molester. That was my first introduction to the sordid side of life.

Soon after that incident, my grandparents and Uncle Roy came to live with us on the ranch. He was only four years older than me, and I thought of him as a brother. Conversely, he thought of me as a pest. I followed my uncle wherever he went.

On a Saturday night, when the generator was fired up and all the adults were playing cards in the dining room, Roy and I were in the bedroom. The head of his bed was pushed up flat against the wall, while across the small room a chest of drawers separated the foot of my bed from the same wall. Roy was sitting on the edge of his bed cleaning his rifle. I was sitting on the end of mine in front of him and a little to the right.

I watched as he ran the cleaning rod up and down the barrel of his gun. I loved the metallic smell of cleaning fluid brushing against metal. That .22 rifle was Roy's pride and joy. Dad had given it to him and taught him how to use it.

When Roy finished cleaning the barrel, and had put all the parts back together, he lifted the rifle and aimed the empty muzzle at me.

He knew better, Dad had taught him muzzle control, but he was so sure the gun was unloaded that he ignored the rule. I pretended to be scared, but I knew as well as Roy did, that the rifle was unloaded. I lifted my hands and wiggled my fingers as though in fright and started falling back on the bed. At that instant, while I was still midair, a shot rang out.

The house fell into an abrupt an eerie silence.

When I looked up, a swoosh of air left my lungs. A bullet had bored a hole right through the chest of drawers and into the wall. The only thing that had saved me from having that bullet plow through my body was the action of falling back on the bed.

Roy's wide eyes met mine, and a moment later we heard the sound of chairs being scooted across the linoleum-covered wood floor. Adult feet came stomping through the door to our room. Roy's rifle privileges were taken away from him for quite a while, and I learned that things aren't always what they appear to be. To this day, none of us can figure out how that unloaded rifle had a bullet in it.

Thinking about the incident now, while I return to the warmth of the car, makes me chuckle.

I first told Cat of the shooting incident years ago when all our children were still in school. Cat was cleaning his rifle and showing it to a friend. I didn't like the way the muzzle of his rifle kept pointing at people, so I told him about my Uncle Roy and warned him to always treat a weapon as if it is loaded.

Skeptical of my story, Cat said he was absolutely sure his gun was unloaded. To prove the point, he aimed the muzzle at the ceiling and pulled the trigger.

You guessed it . . . the gun went off!

To my credit, I never said, "I told you so," but I sure gave him the eye, and it was great fun, thereafter, to hear my husband grumble whenever some visitor looked up and asked, "What happened to your ceiling?" It was a lesson well learned.

A well-learned lesson for me, as well as another defining moment, happened right after the shooting incident with my uncle Roy. My best friend and I liked to walk to the store after school, in the time before the bus picked us up. There was only one store in Fort Jones, but it carried a little bit of everything on its shelves. Sometimes Kathy and I bought a candy bar or a coke, but most often we just looked at all the things we wished we could have but couldn't. Money was tight back in those days.

Whenever we entered the store I migrated to the shelf that held plastic horses. There I would imagine owning one of those plastic beauties and dream of it sitting on my shelf at home. The one I wanted most was a pinto. On this particular day I grabbed that plastic pinto when no one was looking and stuck it in my book bag.

I had completely forgotten our parents were coming to the school for a special meeting. I spotted my father as Kathy and I were walking back across the open field that separated the school from the store. I made some kind of excuse and was able to shift the plastic horse into Kathy's bag.

Though I rarely told a lie, I told a lie that day.

I reasoned that Kathy's father was a pastor of a church and she wouldn't get into much trouble. I, on the other hand, received a whipping every time my father returned home, and sometimes for things I didn't even do, so I figured this evil deed would earn me the biggest whipping of all time.

When accused of stealing, I pointed my finger at Kathy and stuck by the lie.

Several times over the next few months I wanted to confess to the truth, but I never did. That guilt of stealing and telling a lie and betraying my best friend stuck with me. Every time thereafter, when I was accused of something, I accepted the guilt, whether I was guilty at the time or not, because of that one defining incident.

My next defining incident happened when I was ten years old and we moved to Woodland, a small town near Sacramento, California. My grandmother had recently bought into religion and invited Momma and me to a Billy Graham meeting. My family did not attend church, but we were excited about seeing this popular evangelist in person. At the end of the meeting I went forward with thousands of other people to accept Jesus as my own personal savior. I wasn't quite sure what that meant. In fact, I failed every one of the mail-in courses the Billy Graham Evangelistic Association sent me. Yet, I believed in God, and Momma and I both started going to church.

Billy Graham had talked about how God was a Father who loved us, but I saw a different view through attending church. God seemed more angry than loving, and I kept thinking about that plastic horse I stole and how I had betrayed my best friend. I figured God must be very angry with me. In fact, I believed I must have committed the unforgivable sin my grandmother always talked about.

Something else happened that same year.

A gang of older boys singled me out from my girlfriend when we were crossing through a park. One of the boys grabbed my shoulders and tossed me to the ground as if I weighed nothing at all. Then the entire group of boys circled over my body. I still remember their leering faces and the sickening smell of their sweat as they started to reach for me.

I screamed and kept right on screaming while my girlfriend ran away. I thought she was going for help but, instead, she ran for home, leaving me to my fate. Help came at the last possible moment, but not at the urging of my friend. She never said a word about it to anyone, and I never spoke to her again.

From that day on I became an invisible girl . . . but not invisible enough.

We moved to Southern Oregon when I was in the sixth grade. First, we lived in Medford, three blocks away from Lincoln Elementary School. There, one boy constantly gave me trouble. When the going home bell rang each day, I would slink through the halls and make sure he wasn't looking before I made a mad dash for home. But then one day, I had to stay after school and talk with the teacher.

Even though I was shy, I tried to keep that teacher right on talking until I was sure the troublesome boy must have already gone home. After the meeting, the teacher disappeared into the faculty room while I tiptoed through the halls and peeked out the back door. Everyone had already cleared out of the schoolyard, so I figured the going was safe. I didn't get far when the boy popped out from a bush and grabbed me from behind. My books fell to the ground as he pinned my arms to my sides.

I tried to break away and run, but he was too strong. He smelled of greasy hair and his slobber ran down the back of my neck. I kicked him in the shins, but that did nothing to stop him. He just laughed and held on tighter.

Then out of nowhere another boy appeared.

The second boy kicked my attacker and then kept on kicking and hitting, first a right, then a left, then another right. I knew the second boy's name, because it was the same as one of the former presidents, John Adams.

John Adams and the bad boy were both connecting hits. I stood there with my mouth open while blood ran down both boys' faces.

"Run!" John Adams yelled.

Suddenly my feet started moving, and they didn't stop until I ran through the front door of my home. When I looked back, the bad boy had already reached our gate. His mouth was twisted in a big smile.

Dad was sitting in his chair by the front window and saw the boy. He turned to me and, while I tried to catch my breath to explain, I noticed the strange expression on my father's face.

He said, "Who's that? Your boyfriend?"

The inflection in his voice was different than I had heard before, and a wave of shame washed over me. I wasn't sure what had caused the shame, but it seemed as if I had done something bad.

No words would come out of my mouth. Though I was barely 11 years old, and had little understanding of the events, I began to believe I was a bad girl, and the feeling of guilt took root in me.

Dad continued speaking to me, but I missed most of his words until he said, "Where's your school books?"

A new wave of fear swept over me as I realized I would have to find those books or be in even deeper trouble.

"No homework," I lied.

The room began to spin. I couldn't believe I had just added lying on top of all my other sins

Momma was in the room too, but as usual, when Dad dealt with me, she remained silent. She simply undid me with a knowing stare, as if she saw every piece of the guilt I carried.

The strange thing about defining moments is they color your view of everything that happens from that moment on. The incident with the lie regarding the plastic horse gave me a wrong view of God the Father. I believed he was angry with me and that nothing could change that fact. The incidents with the child molester and the gang of boys gave me a wrong view of men in general. I believed they only wanted my body for some sordid reason and that none of them could ever truly care about me as a person. The incident with the bad boy made me believe that guilt can never be satisfied.

John Adams waited for me at school the next day and handed me my rescued books. I looked into his face and realized, for the first time, that a choice was set before me. I could either remember the incident as evil by focusing on the bad boy, or I could remember it as good by focusing on what John Adams did for me.

It was easy to focus on the good while John Adams stood before me. I saw the possibility that some men might see me as a person and not just as a body. I also saw that God must not be as angry with me as I first thought, because he had sent a rescuer to protect me. Choosing to see the good points of a bad situation changed the way the incident molded me. It helped me to rise above the circumstances in spite of what others might think of me.

Now, as I roll up the window of my Ford Explorer against the pounding wind, I realize I need to look for the good in my relationship with Momma. I've certainly been surprised at how many good memories I have of Dad, but as the pounding wind rocks my car, my throat begins to constrict, and I feel as if someone is choking me.

I cannot think of one good memory with my mother.

8

Shield of Mercy

Many would be cowards
If they had courage enough.

—*Thomas Fuller*

2009, Still Thursday afternoon
Lost Creek Lake

I climb out of my car and stand in the wind, hoping the chill will reach through my bones and numb my heart. I am weary of trying to figure out all this relationship mess. I am sure there must be some good memories with my mother, but my brain simply isn't able to conjure them up at the moment.

The wind bellows like an angry giant flapping its arms, spinning the tops of pine trees, and throwing cones and broken limbs to the nearby forest floor. I'm relatively safe where I stand in a treeless parking lot, but I have no protection from the biting cold.

Unlike most people, the storm does not repel me. Instead, the wonder of it calls me away from depression. I stretch out my arms and lean into the wind, thinking of other storms that have drawn me close to the heart of God.

October, 2007
Sky Lakes Wilderness

"You're right," Cat said after I showed him the well-worn trail near our hidden wilderness camp. "This is an elk freeway."

While we stood beneath the canopy of old growth fir, a strange rumbling sound began rolling up the mountain. It sounded like the engine of a large vehicle, but no vehicles were allowed in the wilderness. We stared down the hill, wondering at the strange phenomenon. In spite of the law, I half expected a heavy piece of road equipment to appear, smashing everything in its wake.

"What do you think it is?" I asked Cat.

He shook his head, straining his ears for some kind of clue.

The noise grew louder and nearer, until it took all my self-control to resist the urge to run. Then, when I expected to see some kind of monster breaking out of the trees, an incredible blast of hail stormed our section of forest. If it weren't for the thick canopy above our heads, we would have been pummeled mercilessly. Even so, the noise was so deafening we couldn't hear one another speak, even though we were standing closer than three feet apart.

Within minutes, the storm passed, leaving an eerie shroud of quiet behind. As we moved down the trail, every footfall sent up an echo. There was no way we could sneak up on an elk now. I slung my rifle over my shoulder and retrieved my camera from my pack. At least I could snap some photos. When I stood back up, Cat was well ahead of me and heading right. I was just about to follow when I heard the snap of a twig on the left.

I froze, camera in hand, waiting to see what animal had caused the snap.

Cat continued on down the mountain, not realizing I had stopped. Calling to him would have alerted the animal I was waiting to see, so I remained silent.

A flash of fur, too dark for a deer or an elk, moved across the stream to my left. It disappeared in a tangle of brush and reappeared as it climbed the far bank, pulling itself up with its arms and pushing with its feet. My first thought was that it must be another hunter, but I couldn't figure out why someone would wear such a thick fur coat into the wilderness. I watched until he appeared on top of the bank, and then I knew it was no hunter. It was an enormous black bear.

I looked at Cat, but he was still heading away, so I aimed my camera for a quick shot.

The bear rambled up the creek, turning over every log in its path.

My close-up lens was too close, so I lowered my camera and started untwisting the lens while fumbling through my pocket for a smaller one. Then I realized my problem. If the bear was too close for the close up lens, and he was coming straight for me, shouldn't I be grabbing the rifle?

My breathing turned into short, hard gasps while the rank smell of bear filled my lungs.

Cat finally stopped and looked back.

"Bear," I mouthed.

It was still headed in my direction and hadn't yet seen me. I either had to yell or shoot. I couldn't shoot, because moving to retrieve my rifle from my shoulder would alert the bear to danger. I couldn't yell, because I was supposed to be hunting. Hunting and yelling don't go together.

"Big bear," I mouthed again.

Cat didn't have the same view I had. A stand of trees stood between him and the bear.

"Very big bear," I mouthed a little too loudly. With his head still down, the animal drew near.

Cat raised his rifle, but the bear kept coming. My breath came in short, sharp gasps, and I found myself unable to do a thing. Then the report of Cat's rifle thundered through the forest. I nearly fell in a faint.

The bear was less than 20 feet downhill but never saw me. He stopped, looked in Cat's direction, and then scampered off totally unharmed.

Cat and I searched until well after dark, but found no signs of a wounded bear. Cat couldn't believe he had missed his shot, a rare thing for him.

The next morning, Cat rose early and went looking for the bear. He found it very much alive and climbing a tree. Again, Cat fired and missed. When he returned to camp, he sighted in his rifle and discovered his scope was off by more than a foot, which meant his bullets didn't even nick the bear. He figured he must have hit the scope against a tree and knocked it out of alignment sometime during the storm.

The news made me glad. It was the same bear we saw every year, and I made Cat promise not to shoot him. Our visits to Trapper Camp would be less enchanting without the bear for a neighbor.

Cat saw the bear once more during the same camping trip, but kept his promise to me and let the free-wheeling bear amble away.

Steve Evans, our hunting boss, wasn't so phlegmatic. "Kill the bear," he said. "He's destroying my property."

He referred to the tent the bear had ripped to shreds two years before. Though I was certain it was the same bear, and although I love the taste of bear meat, I still wanted the bear to live. The chance of encountering him had become part of the wonder of the wilderness. Yet, I knew if that bear gave us much more trouble, Cat would put an end to him. Both of us had plenty of experience in wild wonder that could suddenly turn dangerous.

Fall, 1985
Wild and Scenic portion of the Rogue River

Sprawled on my yellow inflatable kayak and nearly falling asleep, I was suddenly awakened to a loud, angry roar, like a hundred lions in battle with as many bears. I looked up to see whitewater pouring over the enormous rocks that formed the jaws of Mule Creek Canyon. It looked like the open mouth of some horrible monster of the deep.

I bolted upright and started back paddling.

John and Gail Johnston, husband-and-wife team, sat in their speeding raft 20 yards in front of me. John shrugged as if to say, "I warned you." Cat maneuvered his own inflatable kayak behind me, along with Gary and Nancy Shaw who made up the rest of our six-person crew.

The force of the water pulled our watercrafts at a furious pace toward The Jaws. John and Gail disappeared behind the thundering mass of white spray. I dipped my paddle hard to the left, then to the right, riding the wave up the side of the rock and through the swirling madness. I dipped again and again, feeling stronger with each dip. Water rushed up and over my kayak from the front. The sound of it thundered off the rocks above me. Then it attacked from the sides and swept across the back. The coldness of it shocked me into a new stage of awareness.

I caught a glimpse of Gail's red vest plunging over the wave in front of me. The yellow of her raft quickly hid her from view. Gail is a quadriplegic with useless legs and only partial use of her arms. When not in a raft, she depends on a wheelchair. I had agreed to this trip because of Gail's bravery. Several of my friends had drowned in the Rogue River, leaving me with a powerful fear of swirling whitewater. Yet I had reasoned that if Gail could overcome her fear in spite of her many limitations, then certainly I should be able to overcome mine. But as the angry Rogue River hurled my kayak toward the sheer face of a rock wall, I wondered if Gail had some kind of courage and strength I didn't have. I paddled hard and willed new strength from muscles I never knew existed. The powerful hydraulics pulled to the right, lifting me high on the crest of a wave. I stuck my paddle into thin air.

Telfer's Rock sprang into sight on the left.

"Dangerous rock and pour-off," John had warned earlier. "People have died there. Avoid it."

My paddle finally found water again.

I dipped and pulled, dipped and pulled until I felt as if I were a part of the river—tumbling and turning, rising and falling to a rhythm as old as the earth itself. The current swept me along, embracing me in its deathly grip until I finally reached the narrows where the whitewater disappeared. With the roar of the river behind me I entered a world of soft quietness where my kayak floated across a smooth bubbling surface. I kept digging, feeling elated, knowing I had made it through Class IV rapids without a single mishap. But this section of Mule Creek Canyon, aptly named "The Coffeepot," was just as dangerous though it appeared less so.

"Keep digging even when you think you're through it," John had warned earlier.

I watched him now in front of me, pulling the long oars of the raft. He turned the boat sideways and looked back at me. I quit dipping for the briefest of moments, just long enough to holler, "Can I stop paddling now?"

It seemed an innocent question, but I should have known better. John was still pulling, after all, even though he looked relaxed while Gail bailed water out of their raft. Too late, I remembered his words of warning when we put in at Grave Creek. He had given us instructions for all the bad sections. He had told us that the Rogue River is 90 feet deep in Mule Creek Canyon, and that some people have been pulled to the bottom never to be seen again.

As soon as my paddles stilled, the river saw its chance and gripped the center of my boat like a giant suction cup, pulling it straight down and scrunching the pointed ends over my head.

What good is a raft, I thought, *if the river can pull an entire inflatable kayak down?*

I imagined myself sinking the entire ninety feet to the river floor where I would join an army of macabre skeletons who had suffered the same defeat.

"Aaaaaaaaggggggh!"

I stuck my paddle furious and hard into the water, pulling with all my might. At first the river resisted, then in one fell swoop, it let go. My kayak popped into the air, and then it came down with a splat!

I plowed the river, sailing past John and Gail as they stared open-mouthed from their raft. I continued to dig, long after we had left the canyon and floated placid water. Swimmers ducked to get out of my way. Divers hollered, "Look out for the crazy woman!" The muscles in my arms screamed for mercy by the time John laid out a tarp for the six of us to spread our sleeping bags on a spit of sand.

"That's your bedroom for tonight," Cat said.

I looked at the open sand surrounding the tarp and the short distance between it and the forest. "What about bears?"

"No problem, as long as we keep everything clean."

I gave him my raised-eyebrows look. Surely the noise and smell of humans would be enough to arouse the animal's curiosity. Cat guided me up the side of the mountain to an outhouse hidden deep in the timber. I spotted an enormous track on the sand in front of the door. "Is that a bear print?"

Cat took a huge step, placing his foot squarely on the track. "Where?" he said.

"Right there," I muttered, pointing at his foot. When he lifted his shoe, all that remained was his own print of a well-worn Nike.

I glared at him.

When I creaked open the door, a ball of dark fur scurried up the mountain and stopped not 15 feet away. With my hand still on the door handle, I held my breath and stared into the eyes of a full-grown black bear. He grunted and pawed at the dead leaves beneath his feet, staring at me, then up the hill, then back at me, then up the hill. His breathing was loud and hard, more a grunt than a breath.

I remembered stories from my youth about people getting horribly mauled by grizzlies and more recent stories of black bears along the Rogue River tearing up boats and threatening campers. Perhaps I would be the first to be attacked. Forgetting that Cat stood behind me, I wondered whether I should run for the river or lock myself inside the flimsy building.

"Just stay calm," Cat whispered.

The bear threw us a few more grunts before erupting into a thunderous roar and running up the hill. The forest opened before him and closed into perfect quietness. It was as if the bear had never been there.

The bear encounter was the subject of dinner as we meticulously cleaned our plates. Later, as we sprawled in our sleeping bags and I stared at an endless array of stars, I thought about the tale of a friend who floated this same river and woke to find a bear sniffing her ear.

Sniffing her ear of all things!

I lay sleepless through the night while Cat snored beside me. I wished he would at least have the courtesy to remain awake. Then I heard a noise—cautious footsteps—making their way down the mountain toward where we slept...at least some of us slept.

"Cat," I whispered.

He snored on.

The footsteps came closer.

"Cat," I tugged at his shoulder.

Nothing.

The smell reached me first, musky and rank. Then I heard the familiar sound of heavy breathing. Just as I opened my mouth to scream, Gail yelled, "Jooooohn!"

I sank on my belly with relief.

The bear tumbled across the sand and ran into the endless black of a moonless forest.

None of us slept the rest of the night. None of us except Cat, that is. He woke for the briefest of moments and went right back to dreamland. I stared at the heavens and listened for grunting sounds above the constant swoosh of the river.

The next day we rose and surveyed Blossom Bar, named not for its colorful foliage but because of the treacherous boulders that blossom at this point in the river. If it wasn't for some clever dynamiting by an oldtimer, we wouldn't be able to get through it at all. One by one, we climbed into our watercrafts and headed out, each of us passing through the Class IV obstacle without a problem.

With the thrill of victory so fresh, we pulled out at the bottom of The Devils Staircase, a Class III rapid. I begged John to let us run the staircase again. What a thrill it would be to ride the rapid without the aid of an inflatable kayak. John was reluctant at first, but finally gave in. Gail and Nancy waited on shore while John, Gary, Cat and I each took an inflatable seat and a lifejacket and hiked back up to the beginning of the staircase. Then we jumped into the churning river, each expecting a delightful adventure.

John jumped first, then Gary, then me. Cat pulled up the rear, wanting to keep an eye on me. We bent our knees and kept our feet out in front as the river hurled our bodies at an amazing pace. Although I wore a lifejacket and kept my arms tucked into the inflated seat hugged close to my chest, the broiling rapid kept my head as much under water as above. Suddenly, a sheer rock wall loomed in front of us.

I forgot that.

A short while ago the river had savagely hurled my kayak straight at the rock face. I had been certain it would smash me to smithereens. Instead, the kayak slithered from high off the rock and made a smooth turn around the left corner.

Now, the river hurled our bodies toward the rock as if we were helpless pieces of driftwood. John slid by with no problem. Gary slammed against the rock, dropped under for the briefest of moments, then popped up and sped off with the current.

I braced myself, taking a deep breath. I was glad I did. There was no jarring pain when I hit the wall, but the river pulled me under and held me. When it finally spit me up, I chugged big gulps of air and choked on water. When I was past the danger, I turned to see how Cat was doing.

I caught a fleeting glimpse of his hands clasped around his yellow inflatable seat. Then hands and seat disappeared at the base of the wall.

"Caaaaat!"

I clawed at the river, attempting a backstroke, but the rapid was too powerful. The roar of it covered the sound of my screams. I kept looking back, hoping to see Cat's bearded face gasping for air. But the empty whitewater continued to churn in complete madness.

Fighting against panic, I kicked my feet behind me and followed the current to our pullout. John and Gary already stood on the shore with their eyes searching the water.

Gail and Nancy sat silently in the beached raft. There was nothing we could do. It would be impossible to get a boat back up the boulder-strewn bank and in the water in time to tie lines and save my beloved husband. We had no cell phones in those days; no way of calling for help; even if we did, it would arrive too late. The hydraulics of the water beneath the wall prevented any attempt at a fast rescue. I felt as if I had plunged into a dream—a nightmare of my own making.

John and Gary and I took a coil of rope and headed back up the bar. We climbed over enormous boulders and prayed to God for a miracle. We kept looking toward the wall for a glimpse of yellow rubber. Nothing appeared. An uncontrollable trembling shuddered across my body. Tears streamed down my face, but I made no sound. I felt incredibly alone, incapacitated as an old woman, hating the river and hating myself for being such a fool by jumping into a major rapid for the mere sake of a thrill.

Neither Gary nor John spoke. The three of us simply stood there, staring at the water, willing Cat to appear. It was the most helpless feeling I have ever known. Life had suddenly lost all meaning and purpose. I choked back sobs as I thought about jumping back into the water and joining my husband beneath its churning surface.

"Lord, save Cat," Gary said. It was the most simple prayer I had ever heard.

Then the impossible happened.

Cat appeared around the edge of the wall. He was not a floating body caught in the current. He was alive! His muscled arms clung to the inflatable seat. My legs turned to jelly as I yielded to uncontrollable sobs.

Cat told us later that the river had slammed him into the wall before dragging him down to the bottom.

"Never fight the river," John had warned us. "It's more powerful than you. Just wait it out. You'll eventually come to calmer water."

Cat had remembered John's words and waited, but the river continued to hold him, as well as his inflatable seat and life vest, on the bottom. When his lungs screamed out for air, Cat clawed his way up the rock wall, using strong muscles to pull himself to a narrow shelf above water where he could breathe. After examining the sheer face of the canyon, he decided the only way out was to jump back into the river. He grabbed the seat and plunged, thinking he would pop around the corner like the rest of us had.

For the second time, the river slammed him into the wall and pulled him under. He used every last ounce of strength to claw his way back out.

The narrow shelf was across the river and hidden from our view. He couldn't see us, and we couldn't see him. This time, Cat sat on the ledge and bargained with God. "You'll have to get me through this. I don't have the strength to pull myself back out again." Then he jumped into the rapid for the third time and miraculously slid around the wall that had attempted to squeeze out his life. He held me in his arms as he told the story.

At that moment, I would have put all our gear on my back and hiked miles out of the wilderness.

I hated the river. I despised the absurdity of its unrelenting power. Yet, it was my own selfish love of adventure I really despised. I spent the night in Cat's arms, soaking up the life and smell of him and thanking Creator Redeemer for being merciful.

9

Long Way Home

We've got a long way to go,
But we've also come a long way.

—Pastor Alistair Begg

October 2009, Thursday evening
Lost Creek Lake

Folding my arms across my chest to ward off the cold wind that has calmed to a breeze, I begin pacing back and forth trying to figure out the impossible love question. Thinking of how I almost lost Cat, I realize it is important to keep short accounts with my mother. Was she telling me the truth when she said she loved me but didn't like me? If I unpack that sentence, I would say my mother doesn't like me.

That kind of truth and knowledge does not set me free as so many Christians claim it will. I believe the verse, ". . . the truth will set you free," has been sorely mistranslated. Instead, this kind of truth condemns me as one who is not likeable. After all, if your own mother can't like you, then who can?

When Momma said she loved me, I believe she meant it. The problem came when she followed that statement by saying she didn't like me. In my mind the last phrase nullified everything that went before, because I cannot understand how both statements can be true at the same time.

What about her other statement, "I think you feel the same way."

Do I love my mother?

"Of course I do," is my first reply.

Do I like my mother?

I like Momma's feistiness and stubborn strength. I like the way she has remained true to my father for over 60 years. I like the fact that she prays for me and the rest of our family and always remembers our birthdays. I like her sense of humor and graciousness with those she loves. I like the way she puts herself together. I like her quick wit and mind.

Yet there are also things I do not like about her. I don't like the way she has never accepted Cat as a true father to all my children, both the ones he adopted and the ones who carry his blood. I don't like the fact that she doesn't recognize what a great, kind man he is, though we've been married for nearly 40 years. I despise the way she continues a relationship with my ex-husband who tried several times to take my life. I don't like her making me guess at her needs or the way she holds back the truth, and I don't like her thinking that being strong means it's better to yell than cry.

So, I come to the conclusion that there are both things I like about my mother and things I don't like. Yet my love for her remains constant.

How strong is that love? That I cannot answer, nor do I need to. Creator Redeemer has only given me two commandments. One is to love God and the second is to love others. It is a process, not an event, and there's always room for growth.

I feel a bit better having worked through the question in a good way, yet part of me is still hanging on to the I-don't-like-you phrase. I hope Momma doesn't really mean it. I hope she means there are *some* things she doesn't like about me.

I admit that I'm a mess of a person. I'm always late, no matter how hard I try to change; I'm drifty as all get out; and I never wear the right clothes or create anything that resembles a hairstyle. I cry too easily and too often, and I can be as stubborn as a ground squirrel. I forget birthdays, rarely call, miss the obvious, laugh in all the wrong places, and say the strangest, embarrassing things off the top of my head.

On the other hand, I'm as loyal as a hound dog and will drop everything to meet a friend's need. I pray with passion, offer hospitality to whoever comes to my door, and I guard my faith and marriage above all. Some people call me a woman of courage; others think I'm braver than I really am. So, why can't my mother find something to like?

A flood of unwanted memories washes through my mind. This is no cleansing stream, but a flashflood of thick, polluted water. Images of when I wished Momma had protected me when I was a teen. My adult mind tells me I'm being unreasonable, that my mother didn't even know I needed protection, but the memories continue to roll. I see another image of me following Momma from the baby ward after the birth of my twin granddaughters. I call to her retreating back as she nearly runs through the hall and enters the elevator. She doesn't even look up as the door closes. I rush down the stairs and catch her in the parking lot. I call out to her, but she climbs into her car and slams the door, without once acknowledging my existence.

Recalling that memory sinks me into despair. She wasn't speaking to me at the time, because my middle daughter had run away from home and Momma blamed me for it. Later she understood that our daughter's bad choices had nothing to do with a lack of love at home, Cat and I loved our daughter as we did all of our children, but the damage was already done. I felt rejected and abandoned.

I feel rejected and abandoned now just thinking about that memory.

That's the problem with a pointing finger; the pointer always has three fingers pointing right back at themselves. I'm pointing the finger now and I know it. I'm doing it because the finger was first pointed at me, but where does it all end?

I know the answer to that one. It ends at the cross, by laying down my rights and desires. It is in losing my self-identity that I will discover the amazing truth of what Creator Redeemer has planned for me. His plans stretch far beyond anything I can dream.

Peace washes over me and the anger and fight are gone.

It's that simple. I still have no answers, no understanding, yet my arms are no longer folded across my chest. They hang in submission at my sides, and I let out a long sigh of relief. None of my circumstances have changed, yet I feel a physical difference.

A full moon has risen on the other side of the lake. Moonlight turns the decreasing white caps into sparkling jewels washing up onto the beach. The sand on the beach is silver white and glowing. It's an incredibly lovely sight, and the sound of washing waves creates a musical harmony with the wind. I can't recall seeing the sun go down, yet a crimson sky kisses the mountains. I lift my arms toward the heavens and thank Creator Redeemer for a gift I do not deserve.

I join the wind in singing a song of praise and worship.

Much later, I return home and eat a meal of cold, leftover tacos while I watch a video I rented a week ago. The movie about does me in. It's called, Big Fish, and it's about a man whose father tells tall stories and is dying. By the end of it I'm bawling my eyes out. How could I have ever thought I could rush into the wilderness to meet my own needs while my father is down in the valley fighting for his life?

I cry myself to sleep, knowing that in the morning I will return to the hospital. Whether it is a safe place or not, it is the place where I am most needed. My father needs me to be there beside him, to encouragement him to fight this battle with every ounce of his strength. My mother needs me to be there for her, to keep the night watch that she is physically unable to keep, and to stand by her decisions no matter how difficult they are to make.

My tears turn into a prayer as I ask Creator Redeemer to give me strength. The whisper and smell of his sweet breath is the last thing I remember before falling asleep.

Momma and Dad, 1947

Me and Dad, Camp Pendleton, California, 1952

Me and Momma, Oroville, California, 1951

Nipper and me on the Scott Valley Ranch between
Fort Jones and Etna, Northern California (1954)

My favorite picture of Dad on top of Lady.
Scott Valley Ranch (1954)

Me and Cat, Arcata, California (1972)

Me and Cat, Trappers Camp (2003)

Part Three
Emotional Leave

I have no need of a bull from your stall
or of goats from your pens,
for every animal of the forest is mine,
and the cattle on a thousand hills.
I know every bird in the mountains,
and the creatures of the field are mine.

—*Creator Redeemer*

10

Sidetracked

By the rivers of Babylon we sat and wept
when we remembered Zion
There on the poplars we hung our harps,
For there our captors asked us for songs . . .

—Jews in exile

October 2009, Friday, October 9
On the way back to the hospital

The morning star hangs high, but the sun is still below Needle Rock when I head back down the mountain and into the valley. I pull into a gas station to purchase needed fuel. I'm proud of myself because I have a folded $20 bill in my purse to give to someone. The gas station attendant looks as if he's seen better days, and I want to give him the 20 bucks without embarrassing him with a handout.

Holding out the folded bill, I say, "My Dad always loved it when people tipped him when he was a gas station attendant. I would like you to have this as a way of thanks for good service."

The man smiles and nods. When he reaches out to accept the bill, his smile grows bigger. I feel good about having done the right thing in the right way, but it also makes me sad. I fear Dad will never get the opportunity to receive any kind of tip again.

Momma is at the hospital when I arrive. She has been here all night. Dark circles have formed beneath her eyes, and she stumbles when she tries to rise from the bench. I urge her to go home and get some rest, but she shakes her head.

When I look at Dad, I cannot believe what I see. His entire body has swelled up like some kind of hideous parade balloon, and a rancid odor I can't quite name fills the room. I scurry to the nurse on duty. After checking Dad, she darts back to the hallway. I know something is wrong.

Momma's rubbing Dad's hands as if she can rub all that swelling away. The same tired mantra pours out of her mouth. "I'll be okay, honey. You can go."

All my good intentions fall away. I try to hold my tongue, but words pour out. "Hang in there, Dad," I say a little too loudly.

The nurse returns with the doctor. Of course, he has three or four students in tow. He's not the kind of doctor who will sit down and talk with patients and their families. He's a young specialist who was brought here from another state to work day and night for a couple of months, and then he'll get time off before working in a different hospital. He's good at what he does, but I think he could use a course or two in the social sciences. Dad appears to be more a challenging problem to be solved than a person to be valued, and we family members are simply in the way.

I try to stay out of the doctor's way as much as possible. I scoot to the far side of the room and sit on the bench. Of course, I'm praying silently. A glance at the chart on the wall where nurses keep a daily tab show me that Dad is well over 200 pounds, and it looks as if most of it is water.

Dad is not a tall man and he's always been proud of keeping his weight just right. There's talk of his kidneys shutting down and a lot of technical stuff neither Momma nor I understand. To give the doctor credit, he throws a few words at us in explanation. He doesn't stay long. He tells the nurse what to do, then he moves on to the next patient. I get the impression that as long as we are all good little machines with promise of performance he'll take care of us.

I hate myself for my thoughts; they're not kind at all. No wonder Momma doesn't like me.

Dad is almost asleep when Momma wakes him again to let him know that it's okay for him to go. I wish Dad would sit up, throw his legs over the side of the bed and surprise everybody by walking out of here. That can't happen of course, because the respirator tube is still in his throat.

The nurse gets help from another nurse and technician. They start moving equipment, and the room quickly becomes too small. Momma unfolds herself from the side of Dad's bed. She doesn't even glance my way as she says, "I'm going home now, Sandra."

She smiles at one of the nurses and thanks her for taking good care of her husband.

I rise and follow Momma into the hall. "How are you getting home?"

She keeps moving, her eyes focused ahead, and I remember that other time when she ran from me after the twin's birth. I stiffen until she says, "Clay brought the car down for me."

She looks too tired to drive and I tell her so, but that just makes her walk faster.

"I *know* how to drive, Sandra."

She could have fooled me. My mother hardly ever drives. I was surprised she drove herself to the hospital after the ambulance picked up Dad and brought him here. I wonder what other surprises wait ahead.

I return to Dad's room and sit by the window as far from the nurses as possible. This life-and-death struggle combined with heightened family issues wears heavily on my soul, and it occurs to me that I'm not even asking the right questions.

When the nurses complete their tasks, I pull a chair over and sit next to Dad. His arm is outstretched beside him on the bed. I slip my right hand into his open right hand as if we are giving each other a handshake. His fingers feel like little sausages, and he doesn't acknowledge my touch, but the closeness calms my soul, and so I sit there for two hours without saying one word.

I've heard it said that a person's life flashes before them when they have a near death experience; I've learned that to be true firsthand, but I never heard that it happens when you're facing a loved one's death. It makes perfect sense, though, when you think about it, and I have lot of time to think about it.

Fall, 1965
Southern Oregon College

They didn't call it date rape back in the sixties. They called it flirting and getting what you asked for.

I was, indeed, flirting, but I didn't ask for what I got. I yearned for the touches that would make me feel as if someone loved me. I wanted the closeness that would come from such a relationship. What I got instead, was pregnant, and that by an alcoholic I could never marry. I had already been around too many alcoholics during my young life.

To make matters worse (if that were possible), my mother had predicted this would happen. I had called her by phone earlier in the school year, hoping to gain some motherly advice.

"I feel as if I'm losing control," I said. "It's like I don't even know who I am."

"I was afraid of this," Momma responded. "You're just like your grandmother."

Without bothering to say goodbye, I hung up the phone and leaned against the prettily papered wall of Susanne Holmes dorm. The aroma of scented candles made me dizzy. I knew what Momma meant when she said I was like my grandmother.

I loved my grandmother Lela, but she had been a prostitute in her younger days. One time she explained to me about how difficult it was being married to an alcoholic.

"He drank all of our money," Grandma told me. "He even sold the coat the kids bought him for his birthday just so he could get another bottle of booze."

I heard the story many times and it never changed, but I also heard my mother's story of how she and Dad had to hock everything they owned to get Grandpa out of jail after my grandmother had him arrested. So, I knew what my mother meant when she said I was just like Grandma. She meant I was a loose woman, the kind that sleeps around with men.

I wasn't at the time, in fact, I hadn't ever been with a boy in that way. One night, while alone in my dorm room, I even told God how Proud I was of myself.

"I'm a pretty good person," I said. "I think I'd be just as good even if I wasn't a Christian."

I don't know if I heard it aloud or in my head, but the answer was as clear as if it had been spoken.

Oh, you think so?

I actually ducked. My first thought was that a lightning bolt might spring out of the sky and strike me dead. It didn't, but the feeling of doom stayed with me, and thus the phone call to my mother.

I was already on the outs with my parents. Dad didn't think a girl needed college, and Momma was mad at me after finding a note in my Bible regarding some issues I had with Dad. I was ashamed of that note, but the words were true, and I didn't know where to turn. There were no safe houses in Southern Oregon in those days, and I lived a lot of my life in fear. It would have been nice to sit down and talk with someone about it.

I don't remember where the relationship between Dad and me started deteriorating. Things seemed okay up until the time I read an article in *American Girl Magazine* about a cheerleader who was worried about what people thought of her. That article astounded me. I thought popular girls never worried about such things.

The next day at school, I was my quiet, mousy self, as usual, but I lifted my eyes from the floor while moving through the halls during class breaks and, sure enough, I discovered that everyone else, especially girls, were so busy worrying about what others thought of them that they didn't even look at me. From that day forth I became a friendly person. Too friendly, according to my father, and maybe he was right. I felt like some kind of caged animal that had been set free.

I discovered a whole new world, where people responded when I reached out to them. A simple word of kindness, laughter at an awkward joke, congratulations when someone did good, all went a long way in gaining a group of friends.

Problem was, I also learned to speak my mind, so where I used to stand mute when Dad would yell at me, I now answered back.

To make matters worse, my body developed early, reaching nearly five-foot-six before I was 11 years old. I felt like a giant, but guys took an interest in my womanly shape. I had no interest in returning their interest, I was still a young girl, though I looked much older. Sometime during my teen years, Dad sat me down and told me there were two kinds of women in the world—the kind a man has sex with and the kind a man marries.

Dad said he thought I might be one of the first kind of women.

I didn't know what to think of those words. They plagued me like a dog worrying a bone. Yet, even with all that, I never had sex with a boy, which brought me to the point of thinking I was a pretty good person ... until those dangerous words of pride spoken to God.

I don't know why my mother's words about me being like my grandmother sunk me so badly, but they did. I felt unlovely and unloved and totally out of whack with society. So, when a popular football player took an interest in me, I responded. But, like I said earlier, I wasn't looking for sex. I was looking for love.

I tried to tell that to Dad when I finally confessed about being three months pregnant on my eighteenth birthday. Momma took to her bed, and even our family doctor blamed me for her breakdown.

"Did you enjoy your date?" The doctor asked me following a prenatal checkup.

I didn't answer, but the memory of that night flashed like a nightmare in my mind. I had tried so hard to get the guy to stop, but he was big and very strong, and none of my screaming or scratching helped. It was as if I was throwing marshmallows at a raging bull.

I didn't share my thoughts with the doctor, of course, it wouldn't have helped. He would have simply accused me of being a flirt. I *was* friendly, after all, so I must have been asking for trouble.

Jay, a boy I had dated in high school for three full years, had asked me several times to marry him. My father counseled me to get back with Jay and not tell him about the pregnancy. Instead, I told him the truth, and he still wanted to marry me. He explained that he had had sex with other girls, so my indescretion was no problem to him.

The whole world was going crazy back then. A war that the news called a conflict raged in Vietnam, and Jay had just joined the service. So my baby boy was born in Balboa Navy Hospital in San Diego, California. I named him after the man who married me, because I was so grateful for his kindness. Too soon I learned that I was his trophy wife, someone he could show off, because I was cute in those days and he made sure I dressed so that other men would notice. In our six years of marriage, I always felt indebted to Jay, but never truly loved.

Little Jay was born with a cleft lip and palette. He was beautiful to me, but others had a problem with his birth defect. Doctors asked me to wait until Little Jay was three months old to perform the needed surgery. They explained they would get better results after he gained more weight.

One time, weeks before the surgery, a lady removed the blanket I had laid over Little Jay's stroller after I warned her to leave it alone.

"The child is too hot under there," she insisted.

The blanket was lightweight and not touching "the child," so I knew Little Jay was fine, but the lady soon wasn't. She whipped off the blanket and fell over in a dead faint. I left her there on the floor of Sears Shopping Center while I whisked my son away.

"Your baby was born with a birth defect," my father once told me, "because of your sin."

He was referring to a verse in the Bible, Exodus 34:7, about the iniquities of the fathers being visited upon the children's children unto the third and fourth generation.

After hearing my father speak those words, I thought of them often and, as I looked at my baby so sweet and innocent in my arms, I vowed I would never have anything to do with a God like that.

That kind of thinking was one of many misconceptions I believed until years later when I started reading the Bible for myself. Then I discovered the truth about God was actually found in the same passage my father quoted. The preceding verses speak of a compassionate and gracious Creator Redeemer who is slow to anger and abounding in love and faithfulness, and who is ALWAYS willing to forgive wickedness, rebellion and sin. He maintains love to thousands!

I suspect my father didn't tell me about those verses because he didn't know about them himself. He was simply quoting what had been quoted to him. We are the ones who pass along our own unbelief and misunderstanding while Creator Redeemer offers to forgive us at any moment. But I didn't know these things at the time, and I believed the lie.

For ten long years I walked away from God.

11

Search and Rescue

The best reason for doing right today
...is tomorrow.

—Pastor Jon Courson

October 9, 2009, Friday
Dad's hospital room

It feels strange to be sitting with Dad and thinking about the bad times we had together when he has no way of sticking up for himself. I have questions to ask him, but the truth is that I would probably not ask the questions, even if Dad were awake. What good purpose would the asking accomplish?

Dad was a different person back then, and so was I.

Since that dark decade I have learned many of the things I've been told about God are not the truth about God. I'm convinced my father learned that lesson as well. That's one of the reasons I call God Creator Redeemer, to get away from those angry-old-man views a lot of us held for too long.

I made a lot of wrong choices, and I am sure to make more, but the past cannot be changed. Looking back on it, I can see the moments that caused me to start going wrong. One such moment was when I brought home a

Junior High School report card where I had gotten all A's except for one B+. Dad had looked at that report card and raised his eyebrows and said, "What's this B doing on here?"

Another time, I cleaned the entire kitchen, determined to pass Dad's military-style muster. I emptied drawers, inserted new shelf paper and even washed the ceiling. The kitchen smelled of lemon wax and Lysol when Dad returned home. He looked around for a long while, and then he walked over to the phone hanging in a wall cradle and wiped his finger across the top of it. It came back coated with dust.

Without saying a word, he held out that finger for me to see. Then he walked away.

That was it for me. The man was impossible to please, so I gave up trying.

Many years later, I asked him why he was so hard on me. I'll never forget the pained expression on his face, as he explained that he had never had a real family and that he raised me in the best way he knew how.

"I thought it would make you better if I pushed you harder," he said, "but I was always pleased with you."

Goodness! That was news to me.

A few years back I traveled to Oklahoma with Dad, and I finally understood a bit of his reasoning. His sister, Colleen, told me that a neighbor had found 12-year-old Dad living by himself and starving while his father was away somewhere for who knows how long. The neighbor hooked up Dad with a job milking cows in exchange for room and board, or neither of us might be here in this hospital room today.

The thought makes me squeeze Dad's hand, but he doesn't squeeze back.

I have to get up and move to the window seat when the nurse returns for her hourly check. Rain clouds fill the sky, so I turn my face to watch them and think about Dad's words that he had always been pleased with me. It sure would have been nice to hear those words back when I needed them. Still, it was nice to hear them when they finally came, and I am ashamed I held that silence against him for so long. I can't change those wasted years, but I can learn from them and work to change the future between Momma and me.

Revisiting the I-don't-like-you conversation, I decide to turn it upside down. What if Momma was really asking me if I like her? When she said, "And I think you feel the same way," perhaps what she really meant was, "I don't think you like me."

Put that way, her saying she didn't like me was simply a response. The thought almost makes me giggle. Sounds like a couple of kindergarteners having a spat.

As a Christian, I have a very real enemy, and he is a liar and a thief and a destroyer. The Bible says to resist him, standing firm in the faith. So, right here and now, I make a pact with Creator Redeemer to believe my mother loves me, no matter what she says or does. I'm determined to believe that anything else is a lie.

I've seen this series of action and reaction before in relationships with other people. When they did or said something to hurt me, it was often because I first unknowingly did or said something to hurt them. Cat has asked me more than once if I realized what I had just said to someone. He will tell me the exact words I said, and I will retort, "But that's not what I meant."

These days I think most of us aren't even speaking the same language. It may be English, but we often hold totally different meanings to words. A glance at a dictionary will prove my point. Look and see how many different definitions we give to a single word. Top that with the fact we have lost the art of listening, and it is easy to see why Momma and I are misunderstanding each other in this time of emotional turmoil.

I determine to make an effort at changing my relationship with my mother into a better one. After all, Creator Redeemer not only created me while I was yet in my mother's womb, but he also redeemed me so that he could make me into a new creation.

When the nurse leaves, I return to my position next to Dad and assure him that I will take care of Momma if anything happens to him. He opens his eyes and looks at me, and I think he understands.

"I'm sorry for what happened earlier," I say, "but I'm going to do my best to show Momma that I love her."

Dad's expression does not change. The first thing I think is that he must blame me for what happened. It's a silly thought, though, because I didn't do anything wrong. So, here is my first opportunity to choose to believe this thought is a lie from the enemy of my soul. I choose, instead, to believe Dad is simply lost in that drug-induced world where coherent thoughts refuse to come together.

I lean my head on the side of Dad's bed and pull in the smell of clean linen, then I return my thoughts back to those ten long years when I stayed away from God. At the time, I thought God had stayed away from me too, and that is the biggest lie I have ever believed.

1968
Norfolk, Virginia

One of Cat's biggest heartbreaks regarding me is that I was a war protestor. I never considered myself in the Jane Fonda camp, but it doesn't make much difference. For years we couldn't even talk about those days. I was never against the men fighting the war, I knew that most of them were trying to protect us, but I hated the establishment that appeared to be making money by sending our young men off to a war that was never even billed as a war. Most of my friends returned from Vietnam hardened and bitter, struggling with horrendous nightmares and feeling completely cut off from their old lives. Many had to overcome serious injuries, and some never returned at all. And what about the marriages doomed to fail before they even began?

Before Vietnam, I naively thought the government truly was for the people. The warm hand of smiling John

F. Kennedy reached out for mine when he was running for President. He stood above me on a temporary speaker's platform in Rogue Valley's Hawthorne Park. He had dropped to one knee in order to reach me, and I still recall the tangy smell of his cologne. From that moment on, I believed every word he said.

Then the terrible news came while I was sitting in math class my junior year of high school. A radio program suddenly blasted over the loudspeakers. At first, neither the teacher nor us students knew what was happening. We heard shouts and someone crying and a lot of commotion. Then someone shouted out, "Oh my God!"

Finally, a strong voice rang over the airwaves. "Ladies and gentlemen. President Kennedy has just been shot."

"Good!" shouted one ridiculous student.

Then the room fell to complete silence.

The principal might as well have sent us all home, because none of us were good for anything the rest of the day. We shuffled through the silent halls like zombies. I wondered about the girl who had yelled out, "good." How could a person hold that much hate in their heart?

I wanted peace and love to rule, and so, apparently, did most of my generation. A rock group called, The Beatles, sang songs about it. I grew my hair long, wore hip hugger bellbottoms and bikini tops and passed out flowers in the park. I said, "I love you," to everyone I met. When we moved to Norfolk, Virginia, I joined a protest group.

I was still married to Jay and, though he was in the Navy, he had no problem with his hippie wife joining the protest. He served his mandatory time in Vietnam offshore, and never saw himself as a killer. I never saw the soldiers as killers either. I was simply mad at a government who wouldn't let our young protectors do what they needed to do in order to protect us and their own lives.

Things changed drastically, one weekend, when the leader of our group formed a gorilla theater and gave their presentation on the courthouse steps. I don't remember what trial was happening at the time, but it was a big one, and our little group made national news. I wasn't there, because I worked at the Institute of Urban Affairs at Old Dominion University, but I heard about it soon enough. Several of the members of the gorilla group came in cheering. I broke into tears when they told me about the demonstration.

One person played the part of a Vietnamese mother with a young child. Another person played the part of an American soldier who struck down both mother and child in cold blood.

I dropped to my chair and put my face in my hands when I heard the story. Two of my uncles were fighting in Vietnam. Both were courageous men serving their country and us. Many of my friends were over there too. None of them would have done what the gorilla theatre depicted. One friend I knew was nearly kicked out of the Marines because he didn't think he could shoot a child who was coming at him with a grenade. I remember him bawling buckets of tears while flipping hamburgers at Arctic Circle Drive In between Boot Camp and his tour of duty.

Cheers rang out when the protest leader returned to campus. I was right there in the hall waiting for him, and we argued for nearly two hours straight, neither of us convincing the other of our views. I ripped the poster I had made off the wall, and that was the end of my being a war protester, but it is a black mark on my life I cannot change.

I was in a Navy hospital in Portsmouth, Virginia, having just given birth to my second son, Rob, the day Martin Luther King Junior was shot. Silence filled the ward of 20 women like that of a funeral parlor. It took a lot of planning to arrange my return home from Portsmouth to Norfolk to fit in with the government curfew. I never imagined a curfew happening in an American city. If we weren't inside our homes shortly after sunset, we could be arrested.

It seemed so foreign, like something that only happens in third world countries.

While in the hospital, several black women shared the ward with me. We all held hands and cried while race riots were happening outside our walls. Nothing had ever prepared our young lives for such a great loss of freedom. In our eyes, King stood for everything that was right and good. It seemed we had taken an enormous step backward in a city divided between open and closed housing. Coming from Oregon, I had no problem living in open housing—blacks and whites together—and Motown was my favorite beach hangout.

When it was time to nurse our babies, I looked around the room and noted mothers from many cultures—Chinese, Vietnamese, French, Japanese, Hispanic, Black, and White. Several caught my eyes and smiled back. I wondered if there never would have been a race issue if women were in charge. Most of us are born with a mother's heart, after all, and have more than enough love to spread around.

Bobbie Kennedy was our last hope. His death just 63 days later sent a lot of us over the edge. No wonder the hills of Oregon are filled with so many hippies. And no wonder many of us went through a time of giving up on our government.

12

A Faithful Guide

"For I know the plans I have for you,"
Declares the Lord,
Plans to prosper you and not to harm you,
Plans to give you hope and a future.

—Creator Redeemer

October 2009, Friday
Dad's hospital room

It's getting late in the afternoon and other than a couple of trips to the restroom and moving from chair to window bench, I've been right here with Dad. I sat in the window seat and wrote in my journal for a short while, random thoughts and reminders of what God was showing me. Now, I'm back to holding Dad's hand and thinking how much it must have hurt him when I became a war protester. The thought makes me shiver, and then I think of a memory that must have hurt him even more.

I was on my way to Canada at the time and very nearly to prison.

1971
Klamath Falls, Oregon

Jay left the Navy early in 1970 and we ended up in Klamath Falls, Oregon, where he became an Oregon State Trooper. I became the resident hippy at all the Trooper gatherings and gave birth to our third child, Michelle, just before Christmas in 1970. The gulf between Jay and me stretched until it finally grew so wide we couldn't get across it. Early in 1971, Jay moved out of our house, and I had to figure out how to take care of three young children on my own. I decided to look for a night job so I could be with my children during the day.

Night jobs weren't that easy to find back then. My first choice was to work at the hospital, but though I had outstanding secretarial skills and showed up every day to ask about a job, they wouldn't hire me, because my marriage was unstable. So I worked a few months as a cocktail waitress at one of the most popular clubs in town. The only experience necessary was a "nice pair of legs," which I had.

While working at the nightclub, I witnessed knifings, gang fights, and the total breakdown of one of my fellow waitresses. It was probably a blessing in disguise when I was fired for not being able to keep up with a rowdy group of reveler's drink orders. One of the men in the group kept telling me I got the orders wrong, which caused me make repeated trips to the bartender to get them right. I didn't get the orders wrong, but the customer was always considered right.

Funny thing is, I discovered years later that Cat was that rowdy reveler.

The first time I ever stepped into a tavern, I asked for a job. I showed up the next day as a potential barmaid-in-training and, before the evening was over, I was on my own with my boss' instructions, "Handle as many problems as you can on your own. We don't want the police called any more than necessary."

95

I wasn't totally green to the types of problems my new boss was talking about. The difference was I never had to handle any of those problems on my own before. There had always been plenty of bosses over me to take care of them. It also helped that my former boss had an agreement with the local authorities, in exchange for an unknown amount of money, that his establishment could deal drugs across the counter and be assured law enforcement officers would turn a blind eye to their illegal activity and yet step in quickly to handle any problems beyond the establishment's control.

I saw heavy nightsticks used on stubborn skulls on more than one occasion.

I mustered a brave smile as I looked at my new boss sitting at the counter in front of me. Behind him to the left sat an enormous man who would be my first problem. A Klamath Indian nursing a bottle of Cold Duck in the corner would be my second.

I swallowed. "No problem boss. I can handle it."

The words had no sooner left my mouth than the big man thumped his thick glass on the table and hollered for another beer.

"Okay." The boss pointed with his thumb behind him. "The big guy's had enough. Go tell him."

If it weren't for my three preschool children safely tucked in bed and watched over by a trusted neighbor, I would have flung off my apron and walked out the door. But I desperately needed this job, so I straightened my shoulders. My smile was bright when I reached the big man.

I grabbed his empty glass. "How about a wonderful cup of our best coffee instead? It's on the house."

A flash of anger crossed his face so quickly that I flinched. Then he turned and looked at the counter where the boss sat. The big man's entire face crinkled into laugh lines. The transformation was amazing.

"No problem, pretty thing. I'll take a cup of that brew if it's as sweet as you."

His laughter still filled the tavern when I returned to the bar to get his coffee.

The boss shook his head. "Never saw anything like it. No other waitress has ever been able to cut him off." He reached out his hand. "You got the job if you want it."

I shook his offered hand. "Thanks. I want it."

The boss left the counter and slapped the big man on the back with a friendly laugh before he disappeared out the door, leaving me alone to manage the tavern.

I breathed a deep sigh as I poured a cup of coffee and headed back to the big man's table. As soon as I set it down, he stood, placed an enormous hand on the sides of each of my shoulders, squeezed, and lifted me off my feet as though I were no heavier than a sack of potatoes. He carried me like that, with my feet dangling in the air, all the way back to the bar, where he stood me in front of the draft machine. "Pour," he said.

I poured.

He staggered out the door not long after.

I grabbed a wet cloth and started rubbing the already shining counter with a vengeance. A law had recently been passed stating that I could be fined for allowing a patron to leave the tavern with enough alcohol in his system to be intoxicated. But even worse was the fact I could face many years in prison if he hurt someone while driving under the influence.

I stared at the counter where my hand pushed the cloth in circles. My job, the very thing that was supposed to help me provide for my children, might end up being the very thing that took me away from them. The intoxicated man had just gone out the door and probably sat behind the wheel of a vehicle. How one earth could I live with myself knowing I could have stopped the death of an innocent person?

"You did the right thing."

I stopped rubbing and looked up. The Indian had moved from the corner to sit on one of the stools at the counter.

"He won't hurt anyone. He's a walker."

"A walker?"

"Yeah. Lives down the road."

"Now that's the best news I've heard in a long time." I held out a hand. "Name's Sandy."

He looked at my hand but didn't take it. "Cobby here. You got a lot to learn about this place."

I dropped my hand. I could bet on his next words. He didn't disappoint me.

"You don't belong here."

I had heard the same thing from several people while working as a cocktail waitress. It was that Christianity stuff. I just couldn't get rid of it. Though it had been nearly ten years since I had given it up, it still had some kind of mark on me that certain people could spot.

"It's a job." I shrugged. "What can I get for you?"

"Another Cold Duck."

I held his eyes with my own. "You may not think I belong here, but I've been around enough to know that most Indians can't handle Cold Duck. Why not have a draft instead?"

His dark eyes bored into mine, giving nothing away. I was instantly aware of the quiet building. The two of us were alone. Still, I held his stare until he finally smiled and said, "Draft it is."

From that day on, Cobby became my self-appointed protector. He sat at the same stool at the counter and eyed everyone who came through the door. He was there on his stool the night a tall, good-looking man pushed up to the bar and pointed a long finger at me. Loud enough for every ear in the full tavern to hear, he announced, "That woman is going to be mine."

Cobby looked at the cocky man, then back at me. I expected him to tell the guy to bug off like he did with every other man who had pulled a similar dumb move. Instead, he smiled and ordered him a beer.

Of all the nerve. "Where's your ID," I demanded of the tall man.

"You're wasting your time," a customer said. "Cat's been coming in here for a couple of years."

Cat stood, reached in his jeans pocket and pulled out his wallet. He flashed me an enormous smile and handed me his identification, but it was his eyes that grabbed me. They were the same blue as a mountain lake just after sunrise, and they were full of his smile.

"He has sensitive eyes," I would later tell a girlfriend who was totally disgusted with me for not giving more details. Despite my resolve to ignore the cocky man, I found myself wanting to believe the honesty I thought I saw in his eyes.

Honesty? I read his ID and smirked. "Look here," I informed the entire tavern, "You say he's been coming in here for two years, but he just turned 21 this year. Joke's on you."

Laughter filled the tavern. "Buy him another round," yelled one of the regulars. "He deserves it." Everyone thought it was a great joke but me. For a moment, I had been ready to believe this guy was different.

I took my time and waited on other customers before returning Cat's ID. When I finally did, he took it as a sign of interest. "Name's Cat," he said, holding onto my hand as he grabbed the offered ID.

I pulled my hand out of his and went back to work. "Why didn't you cream him?" I whispered to Cobby.

Cobby smiled and sipped his beer. It was interesting that after having appointed himself as my protector, he never once tried to ask me out. He had quite a reputation with the women. He also had quite a reputation for tearing up the town's bars and the people in them. I only had trouble with him once, when I inadvertently served him Cold Duck and he nearly rammed a cue stick right through the middle of a customer. I didn't make that mistake twice.

It wasn't until over a decade later I realized Creator Redeemer had been in charge of our relationship even back then in the tavern. For some reason Cobby saw something deeper in me than just a sexy body, and he simply wanted to see that no harm came to what he thought was a good girl.

Tonight his reaction with Cat intrigued me. The tavern calmed as Cat joined the men in a game of pool. He was sitting at a table when I took him his beer. He stood and towered over me like a ponderosa pine. Then he spread his arms out, hands open.

"Take me," he said, "I'm yours."

I couldn't think of one word to say. But then, I never really had to. For the next few months, Cat became a regular in the tavern. Seemed he and Cobby had struck up some kind of agreement where they would both stay until all the other customers left, then Cobby would say "Goodnight," and leave me alone with Cat. Soon Cat took me out for coffee after work while telling me endless stories.

The only other man I had heard tell stories like that was my father. And Cat's stories, like my father's were hard to believe. Some of his stories seemed far-fetched for a man his age. I was much wiser at the ancient age of 23. Yet, every story checked out, until one fall evening when two of my best friends ordered a beer.

"Got something to tell you," Dixon said, waving me down so he could whisper in my ear. "Cat's saying he's been going to bed with you. Thought you didn't do that?"

Swallowing a sudden burst of anger I snapped, "I don't."

I walked back to the counter where my trembling hands poured their beer. Soon after I delivered their beer, Cat strolled into the tavern, planting himself at the bar.

I marched over to him.

He turned. Surprise registered on his face when he saw my stormy expression.. "What?"

"What's the deal telling people you went to bed with me when it's not true?"

Out of the corner of my eye, I saw my two friends choke on their beer. They bolted to their feet and fled the building, leaving half-empty glasses behind.

Cat followed my surprised gaze as I watched their escape. "Oh, those two," he said. "They're just mad because I gave them orders to do a job."

"A job?"

"At the radar site."

Cat was referring to Keno. He was part of the U.S. Air Force Team stationed there.

"But they told me they worked for the telephone company," I said.

"Sounds about right. Can't believe much those two have to say."

My legs suddenly felt weak beneath me. I left Cat and started filling orders, but my mind was mulling over the fact that my friends, the only two people I had really trusted—the two men who said they would help me and my children find a new home—had been lying to me. Cat was in the Air Force, which meant that if they worked for him, they were also servicemen. They had even told me how they climbed telephone poles and described their work patching lines.

I looked back at Cat.

How much did I know about him? Perhaps it was the way of *all* men to lie and use women for their own benefit. If that was the case, he wouldn't get the chance. That night I left the tavern for the last time and, because it was my policy to never let anyone know my last name or where I lived, I figured it was the last time I would ever see Cat.

Being without a job left me financially unstable and wondering how I would feed my children, but the biggest problem came in the form of more betrayal. My ex-husband laughingly informed me that two of his friends were ready to testify in court that I had gone to bed with them.

"You don't have a chance in the world to win a case against me," he said.

The case he was talking about was his sudden and unexpected desire to gain custody of my children. It didn't make any sense, because one of the reasons he gave me for leaving was the fact that he had been forced to grow up too fast.

"I'm not ready to be a father," he had said.

The fact that he wasn't the biological father of all of my children should have given me hope. Instead, it made me feel all the more unworthy as a mother, but I also knew no one could love my children as much as I did.

Thinking of my upcoming day in court—a seemingly active prostitute against a seemingly upstanding law officer, left me reeling with panic. The next morning I had everything packed in the car, including my three children. Canada was only a little over a thousand miles away. We could go there and start a new life.

I made it as far as the Indian Reservation in Chiloquin before a police cruiser pulled me over. I had no choice but to stop. Pulling alongside the road, I turned off the engine and rolled down the window. One of the two policemen who had planned to testify falsely against me leaned into my window.

Neither of us said a word.

I thought of all the times he had visited our home when my ex and I were together. I had trusted this man.

He looked at me, and then his eyes turned to my three children tucked safely in the backseat with all their favorite toys stuffed between them.

"We're going on a trip," Little Jay said.

The policman cursed, took off his hat, and ran a hand through his hair.

I stared at the windshield, tears streaming silently down my face.

"Go home," he grumbled. "I'll talk with the others . . . and I promise . . . none of us will appear in court."

He slipped his hat back on his head and marched to his cruiser. I watched him leave, and then I turned the car around and drove home. It's a good thing I did, because I learned later that I could have been arrested for kidnapping, and my children would have been left without their mother. Even back then, when I did not acknowledge him, Creator Redeemer was taking care of me.

13

The Elusive Path

I am a follower
Of the Jesus Way.

—*Richard Twiss*

October 2009, Friday afternoon
Dad's hospital room

Dad's eyes are closed now, and I'm glad he's not looking at me. He raised me to have high respect for both law officers and military people, but I lost a lot of my respect after what happened in Klamath Falls. I saw too many things that shouldn't have taken place. Dad doesn't know about those things; I never told him.

When I was young, after Dad moved us from the ranch in Fort Jones, we spent a couple of years in Yreka, California, where Dad was a Deputy Sheriff. He was quite proud of that position and was very good at it, but it came to an end after one night when a false alarm rang out and Dad jumped up to head for his cruiser. The thick glass door did not open as it should have, and Dad's head rammed right through it. The door wasn't made of safety glass, like we have these days, so Dad ended up with an impressive scar right down the left side of his forehead.

I look at that scar now. Every one of the nurses and technicians has asked how he got it. Whenever he's awake and I tell them the story, Dad nods. I know he wishes he could tell it himself. Dad is a great storyteller, and he's lived a life worth telling.

Whenever Dad's awake, I make sure to tell the attending technician about Dad being a Marine. There's a saying that you can take the man out of the Marines, but you cannot take the Marines out of the man. That is certainly true of my father. He was proud of being a Marine and prouder of serving his country in time of war. He did the hard things in order to protect the people and freedom he loves. Because of this, I always send him a thank you note on Veteran's Day.

Leaning over him now, I tell him, "Thank you," and I tell him why. His eyes are wide, but he doesn't utter a sound.

This silence is killing me; I would so love to hear his voice.

My hands smell like sanitizer, otherwise I would think someone had opened the windows and let the wind rush in. The inside air is as cold as the outside air. The doctor has ordered this cold in order to help Dad heal. I reach for my Italian wool shawl and wrap it around my shoulders, and then I continue to hold Dad's hand. It's probably the only thing warm on his body right now, but the medical team has poured enough drugs into him that he's probably not aware of it. After straightening my back into a different position, I continue my journey through time. It seems the best way to pass these long hours, since I cannot focus my attention on a book.

1972
Arcata, California

Several months passed after my planned trip to Canada and my return home before I ran into Cat. When I did, he grabbed me and wouldn't let go. I well remember the day

I realized I loved him. Hot anger had me storming around the house trying to get rid of the feelings that refused to go away. This man had captured my heart and soul. I hadn't planned to ever let that happen, but love snuck up on me until I couldn't bear the thought of facing life without Cat.

"What's wrong?" He stood in the doorway of the kitchen staring at me.

I stared back, trying to muster anger but, instead, I broke down in tears.

He crossed the room in two strides. "Babe," he said, pulling me into his arms. "What's up?"

I shook my head, and then the words tumbled out. "I love you."

Afraid the words would repel him, I closed my eyes so I wouldn't see him turn away, but he surprised me by drawing me closer and whispering in my ear.

"I've been in love with you from the first moment I saw you," he said.

The tears poured again, only this time out of relief.

A month later, Cat and I walked hand in hand into a department store in Arcata, California, where he bought a $20 gold ring. After paying for it, he slipped the single band onto my finger while the clerk wrinkled her nose. Cat didn't seem to notice the clerk's sneer. He kept his eyes on mine.

"This is only an outward sign of what I already feel inside," he whispered.

I wanted to believe his words, but part of me doubted. We had been living together for several months. My father wouldn't allow us in his house because, as he put it, we were living in sin. Our living together sealed Dad's opinion of me as a loose woman, and it filled me with shame. But when I looked at Cat, I felt no shame. I simply felt his love holding me together and giving me strength to face an uncertain future.

"I'll marry you," he promised, "the first moment I can."

My father told me I was stupid to believe Cat, and I often wondered if he was right.

At the time, Oregon law stated that a woman with children could not remarry for six months following her divorce. The law was meant to give couples time to mend their relationship for their children's sake. My ex-husband had moved out long before we could afford to get a legal divorce. I had spent a good deal more than six months trying to mend our relationship without making any headway. None of that time counted toward my six months by law. The counting started after we legally filed for a divorce. Even though Cat and I and my children were starting a new life in California, the Oregon law still held.

While we stood in the department store after he bought me the ring, he said, "A marriage certificate is just paper. Our union is deeper than that."

I stared at the ring as the clerk huffed and turned her back on us.

We left the store and climbed into the U-Haul truck that held everything we owned, which wasn't much. I had let my ex-husband keep the house, the considerable amount of money he had inherited from his father, our brand new refrigerator, and the family dog. My only concern was keeping my children. I had watched enough couples argue and fight over who gets what until both of them were so angry and bitter than no one wanted to be around either of them. I was glad to leave all the stuff behind.

Cat and I drove to meet our new landlady who only accepted married couples with two children. The ring was enough for the married part. She knew about Little Jay and Rob, but she didn't know about Michelle, our third child. I suspect she figured it out soon enough when she came to pick up the rent money and Michelle's cheerful coos wafted from the bedroom. Compassion kept a smile on the landlady's lips as she pretended not to hear.

Others weren't so kind. I could forgive my father, because I knew he was afraid I was one of a long series of women in his life who loved their men more than their children. He had often told me the story of how his own mother had left him as a toddler while she ran off with another man. Her action completely colored the way he viewed women.

I understood that in Dad's mind I had become that kind of woman. What I didn't understand is that Dad's philosophy also colored my thinking. July first, the day I could legally become a wife, came and passed without Cat saying a word to me regarding marriage.

I stared at the ceiling the entire night and became quieter with each passing day. Cat was pulling green chain at the Redwood lumber mill in Big Lagoon in those days, and the bus that took him to work and back stopped Friday nights at a tavern in McKinleyville. Though Cat had no choice but to stop with his fellow workers, I started wondering about what he was doing in that tavern. He returned home from work and greeted me with the same loving kiss, but my return kisses had grown stiff and wary. It was amazing how quickly my trust in him had turned to doubt.

"What's wrong," he would ask.

"Nothing."

Where I once saw love and compassion, I now saw lust. Where I once read concern, I now read patronization. Caring? Flippancy. Honor? Bragging. Fear tainted every emotion. *My father was right. I am a bad woman. How could I have ever thought I could be anything different?*

The lies tugged at the thread of my essence, unraveling every semblance of sanity. I had been in this dark pit before. I had tried to take my life years ago when I first realized what a disappointment I had been to my parents. I had convinced myself the world would be better off without me. This time, I knew my children needed me, so I decided to give Cat until the end of July. If things didn't change by then, I would pack up and leave.

On July 31, the last day of the month, Cat finally demanded to know what was wrong. As soon as I told him, he loaded the children and me in the truck and drove to the Justice of the Peace. He told Little Jay and Rob to wait in the truck, because they thought we were already married. Then he grabbed a secretary in the front office to witness our union. Michelle sat in a pew of the tiny chapel singing songs while the Justice of Peace pronounced us man and wife.

Suddenly my world shot into focus.

As soon as we had that marriage certificate in hand, my father welcomed Cat as if he were his own son. Less than a year later, Cat adopted all three of my children.

"He must really love you," people used to say after seeing all those kids trailing behind us.

Nodding my head, I would wait for the breath of a moment before saying, "Yes. He really does . . . and the love runs both ways."

14

Setting up Camp

Even the sparrow has found a home,
And the swallow a nest for herself,
Where she may have her young
—a place near your altar,
O Lord Almighty, my king and my God.

—The Psalmist

1972
Cascade Mountains, Southern Oregon

It wasn't long after I married Cat that we moved back to Oregon, and in a very short time we found ourselves disconnecting with society. We purchased 12 acres of timbered land bordered by Bureau of Land Management property on three sides. We had high hopes of building our dream home. It would have carpeted floors, paneled walls, and indoor plumbing, a rock fireplace, sweeping porches and wide windows. After checking on rules and regulations with the county, we decided the property was a good place to invest our hard-earned money. Yet, right after signing the deed, the county enforced a moratorium on septic permits, completely shattering our dream.

With no permit, we could get no electricity, we could have no well, we could get no insurance, and we couldn't legally build. Still, we had the deed in hand and were reluctant to give it up. One day while Dad was working the soil on his own property, I asked him for wisdom regarding our building situation.

"What do you think Dad?"

He pushed his booted foot against the shovel, sinking it deep into rich earth. I loved the smell of its life-giving dampness. Then he folded his arms and let his weight rest against the shovel as he peered at me.

"It'll be hard. You'll have to haul water, and you'll have to do something about putting in a road."

I took a deep breath. I had expected him to tell me how silly my idea was, but his answer came quick enough that he must have already put some thought into it.

He said, "Cat's welcome to some free two-by-four seconds from the mill, and you can use particle board for the walls. But you'll have to work fast and get a temporary shelter up before the rains hit."

"So, you think we can do it?"

The backs of my arms were starting to chill. The prospect of building our own home excited me, but I feared for our three young children. We would be far from a doctor or hospital, and there would be no way of phoning for help during emergencies. *But our own home...*

"Pioneers did it," said Dad.

I stared at him.

He stared back. "I don't see why you can't do anything they did."

This was one of the things I loved most about my father. He believed you could do anything you set your mind to, and he wasn't just a man of words. He spent his life proving it. He had built a house for Momma and me when I was little. Momma always jokes about how they went back to see it years later and discovered it had blown over. But it had served its purpose when we lived in it. Because of his thirst for adventure, Dad held so many different jobs over the years that my friends stopped believing me when I told them about it.

"No one could have done that many things," they would always say.

110

"My dad did," I would answer, and then I'd stuff my hands into my pockets and walk away. If they didn't believe me about my father, then they weren't good enough to be my friends. Now my father was giving life to my dream, telling me that Cat and I could actually build our home in the woods.

I called Cat over, and the three of us made plans. We could begin work as soon as the ground hardened enough to drive our one-ton truck loaded with building materials up the steep hill to our home site. Sawing and drilling would have to be done by hand. Falling trees was the first thing on the agenda. We needed enough logs to make a bridge and serve as cross beams for our house. My job was to peel the bark off the fallen logs.

I peeled, Cat built. Cat sawed, I hammered. Seven-year-old Little Jay and six-year-old Rob straightened bent nails and helped their father carry wood. Three-year-old Michelle watched with delight. It was quite the family affair, and all three children hauled rocks while I dug a road out of the steep bank with nothing but a pickaxe and shovel. The road was only be crossable during the summer months; our feet served us well the rest of the time.

The walls of our house went up fast, but the roof had to wait until we made enough money to buy materials. I often wondered if I was the only person alive who had to sweep leaves out of my living room. The first time the sun rose high in the sky, every candle I owned turned to liquid. Kerosene lanterns provided light during the evenings when we read books and listened to myriad sounds of the forest—drumming nighthawks, hooting owls, croaking frogs, yipping coyotes, clicking cicadas—mountain music filled our lives and led us in a search of Creator.

Part of the reason we had fled society and escaped to the hills in the first place, was because of the madness infecting the world in 1972. It was the same year the United States accidentally napalmed the friendly village of Trang Bang in Vietnam, the same year the PLO terrorized the Olympics held in Germany by killing two coaches and taking nine hostages, the same year British troops opened fire on Catholic demonstrators and killed 13 unarmed men. The madness made me yearn to disconnect with society and reconnect with my family roots—my Cherokee grandmother on my father's side who swore she was related to Daniel Boone's wife; my Irish grandmother on my mother's side who read books by moonlight when she was a teenager. Both women loved the land, as did my grandfathers.

My father has always been as much at one with the land as he was with breathing. Dad refused to take any government handouts during three financially difficult years of my childhood, choosing, instead, to hunt and fish and live off the land.

I had believed my reconnection with the land would be immediate and solid. Instead, I found myself quivering over every little sound in the woods. The scream of a cougar quickly turned my thoughts to Bigfoot. I was afraid the enormous hawks flying overhead would take off with three-year-old, Michelle, mistaking her for dinner. Packs of howling coyotes had me reaching for the shotgun. Rattlesnakes had me tiptoeing to the outhouse in the heat of the afternoon sun while I watched for any sign of slithering movement. Rustling night sounds brought me wide awake as I lay frozen and listening. Was it getting nearer? Was it a big footfall, or small? Everything was a threat, including the weather.

The first winter a five-gallon bucket of water froze solid in the room that doubled as living and sleeping quarters. Pulling Michelle into bed with me was the only way to keep her warm. I was sure we would all freeze to death, but we didn't. It was probably the hikes up the hill that warmed us up. We had to park our car a half-mile away at the end of a bumpy road.

Cat worked nights at the lumber mill where Dad was head sawyer. I was never quite sure what creatures would visit at night while Cat was away. One night, a huge wood beetle, as big as my hand, and sounding like something out of a science fiction movie, flew into our roofless house.

I didn't know if I should go for the hammer or go for the gun.

I went for neither, because my dog decided it was great fun to keep that buzzing monster flying. I threw a blanket over my head and screamed for help. The bug kept hitting the blanket, making me scream even louder.

The nearest neighbor lived a quarter mile away. He heard my screams and came to the rescue. I answered the door and peeked from beneath my blanket. He stood there with his shotgun.

I pointed a shaking finger to the monster clinging to the wall.

"You want me to shoot it?" Ron asked.

I thought it might be a good idea except for explaining later to Cat how our wall got riddled with buckshot. Instead, I retrieved a heavy motor's manual from our shelf and had Ron whack the bug with it.

Ron assured me I wouldn't see another of those enormous bugs in my lifetime.

"They usually keep themselves to rotten logs," he said.

After he left, two more of those monsters flew in that very night. I had a lot of explaining to do when Cat returned home the next morning and found me asleep in the car while the kids were still in their beds.

My biggest fear was Bigfoot, especially after Cat lost his job and I started work at Harry and David Packing House in Medford. People throughout Southern Oregon were talking about Bigfoot. They had even set up a trap for him in the Applegate Valley. Sometimes, I didn't get home until two or three in the morning. I nearly ran up that half mile of dark road between the car and our house. My doctor kept asking me what was making my blood pressure run so high.

I didn't fess up about my fear of Bigfoot then, but Doctor Dan discovered the entire story at the birth of our son Clay.

The night before, I had visited the outhouse and was staring into the brilliance of a black cloudless sky. On a mountain night, with no electric lights and no moon, the stars look as if you could reach out and touch them. I was admiring their closeness when, suddenly, not more than ten feet away, the most horrendous, bestial scream shattered the night.

"It was a haunting sound," I told Doctor Dan, "like a woman turned ghost and caught between two worlds."

My dog beat me into the house peeing on the floor in fright. I ran as fast as I could, using both hands and feet to climb the porch stairs.

I *knew* Bigfoot was out to get me.

Cat repeatedly assured me it was a mountain lion, but I didn't believe him. I remained awake the entire night thinking of all the stories I had heard of Bigfoot, especially the ones about entire families disappearing without a trace. I feared something big and awful was ready to pounce at any moment—or worse yet—make off with one of my children.

Finally, a co-worker told me about an inexpensive roll of plastic we could buy. Cat and I stapled it to the rafters for a temporary ceiling. We tacked sample blocks of carpet to the airy pressboard floors and used our small amount of funds to purchase a better wood heater. The changes soon transformed our freezing death factory to the dream home we had envisioned.

My fear was soon transformed as well. I learned we mostly fear what we don't know—mere shadows and sighs. So, the more I became reacquainted with the land, the more I grew to respect and love it.

After tucking the kids into bed at night, I would walk the forest perimeter while staring into an endless array of sparkling stars. As long as the owl hooted, there was nothing to fear. When the forest fell silent, I stopped as well, holding my breath and listening. When the clicking cicadas restarted their song, I restarted my walk, knowing all was safe once again. I carried no weapon, yet I felt no fear. It was a unique time of innocence and beauty.

2009, Friday afternoon
Dad's hospital room

I sit next to Dad and try to pretend I'm back in the wilderness. I imagine the far off bugle of a bull wapiti and the haunting call of a loon, two of my favorite sounds in the entire world. Cat has probably heard them both in base camp this week while I sit here to the constant swoosh of Dad's respirator.

I don't know if the respirator is a good thing or not. Dad didn't want it, he did it for Momma's sake, but if he had gotten his wish I wouldn't be here now taking the time to recall these memories and find some healing for myself. Such as it is, the respirator has provided a connection I wouldn't have had otherwise. So, even though I hate to see Dad suffer, I'm glad he's here a bit longer.

"Thank you, Dad," I whisper. "Thanks for giving me a spirit of wild adventure, and thanks for raising me to believe I could do anything I set my mind to. You've given me a great gift."

A different nurse whisks into the room, throws back the privacy curtain and says, "You need to leave. Visiting hours are over."

Her brusque manner does not surprise me; she's one of the few nurses here I would not describe as "warm." What does surprise me is that her words mean that it is 7:00 p.m., and I've been here the entire day without once eating a meal.

I rise to leave. My right hand is still in Dad's palm and I lay my left on top. "I'll be back soon, Dad," I say. I have to leave for a while."

Dad's eyes shoot open and he grips my hand with a fierceness that startles me.

The nurse is still holding the privacy curtain open, waiting for me to vacate the room.

I glance at her and back to Dad. "I won't be gone long," I try again, "and I'll just be down the hall in the waiting room. These people don't want me here during the shift change."

115

Dad's grip remains strong and he shakes his head.

I sit back down. No one is making me leave now. My father *wants* me here.

Part Four
A Place of Safety

Who let the wild donkey go free?
Who untied his ropes?
I gave him the wasteland as his home,
the salt flats as his habitat.
He laughs at the commotion in the town;
he does not hear a drivers shout.
He ranges the hills for his pasture
and searches for any green thing.

—*Creator Redeemer*

15

Far Seeing Places

There they were overwhelmed with dread,
Where there was nothing to dread.

—*Creator Redeemer*

October 2009, Friday evening
Dad's hospital room

I remain in the chair next to Dad's bed the rest of the night. That one simple action of him clutching my hand lets me know my Dad loves me. The realization takes my breath away.

A team of technicians come and go, but no one tries to make me leave. They too have seen the transformation, though no one understands it.

I don't understand it myself. Why should such a simple action replace all the years of doubt? It has to be a God thing, I reason. We've touched the miraculous, shifted between metaphysical realities without even realizing the change was taking place. Restoration became a reality without a single word being said.

I'm no longer an outcast. I belong.

The thought takes me back to the time when my first restoration took place. It was a restoring of my relationship with Creator Redeemer, and it changed my life from that moment on.

1974
Cascade Mountains, Southern Oregon

Living so close to nature made Cat and me well aware of an involved Creator, one who enjoyed his creation. *God is spirit, and I live and move and have my being in him.* That single revelation brought me to my knees on a sunny summer afternoon.

Staring into the heavens, I said, "God if you're real, show me."

Get a Bible.

The answer wasn't audible, and yet the impression was as strong as a voice in my mind. So strong, I answered aloud. "I've read the Bible before, and I didn't find any answers."

Get a Bible.

The voice was insistent, so insistent that I searched through Little Jay and Rob's room looking for a Bible given to them through their Sunday School. The fact we had taken them to church still surprised me. Cat and I had been sharing dinner with the rest of the crew on the hill, a mix-match of characters who had dropped out of society, when the discussion turned to religion. "Our kids can make their own choices," Cat said.

I agreed.

Rob and Little Jay were playing in a corner of the room and didn't appear to be listening, but their heads popped up and Little Jay said, "We would like to go to church."

The room went quiet.

I looked at Cat. "You take them."

"No way," he shot back. "You take them."

The rest of the crew laughed, telling our boys they were their witnesses. They thought it was the funniest thing that Cat and Sandy would step foot in a church.

Cat and I argued for several weeks before we decided both of us would keep the promise. The church was 18 miles away, but it was the only church I knew of, since I had attended there as a teenager. Cat and I sat in the church parking lot, hand-rolling his cigarettes while our children attended Sunday School. I was pregnant with our fourth child, so when the weather turned bitter cold, we ended up inside the church with the kids. Some folks walked out when they saw us walk in. I wore long skirts that trailed in the mud while hiking from our house to the car and the bodices of my dresses were cut a bit low. Cat's hair fell well past his shoulders. Most of his clothes were either hand-me-downs or were found at second-hand stores.

At first we were merely curious spectators. We attended Sunday School, not staying for the main church service, because we figured it would be far too boring. In the main service everyone sat in pews and just stared ahead. In Sunday School we sat in chairs and were allowed to ask questions.

The pastor was our teacher, leading a series of classes on marriage. Most of his ideas seemed prudish and old fashioned to me. I came from a generation that promoted free love and no ties. Yet, Cat had told me often enough that if he ever found me in bed with another man he would shoot to kill both of us. His declaration didn't sound all that free to me. It sounded exactly like what a lot of men had done for past centuries to take care of such a problem.

One of the things we liked most about Sunday School was the Praise-the-Lord guy. It didn't matter what you said to him, he always flashed an enormous smile and said, "Praise the Lord!"

Cat and I exchanged bets on it, and even brought some of our friends to see for themselves. All this time we were merely spectators, watching from afar.

The turning point came when we arrived one Sunday after Cat picked up our dog and stuck her in the back of the truck. She had followed us down the road after chasing a skunk. Cat didn't have time to walk back up the hill and change, and he didn't much want to be in church anyway, so he marched into the Sunday School room and plopped himself down on the front row. He crossed his arms over his chest just daring somebody to ask him to leave.

I sat beside him, desperately trying to suppress a giggle.

The pastor gave a brave attempt at continuing his lesson, and then he finally loosened his tie and rushed to the windows. He started flinging them open even though snow fell from the sky outside.

"It's hot in here," he said in way of explanation. "I think we need some air."

Of course, the praise-the-Lord buy offered his usual exclamation, only this time most of the people in the room agreed with him, praising the Lord for needed fresh air.

At the close of the class, the pastor hugged us both, while everyone else fled the room.

Later, the praise-the Lord guy and his entire family of six braved the long winding roads leading to our place and trudged up our snowy hill. They were loaded with gifts of groceries and essential items we couldn't afford. There were so many gifts that our neighbors, farther down the hill, had to help the family bring their gifts to us.

How could we not love these folks? There was something different about them. It was at this point that we began to see the praise-the-Lord guy as a real person and called him by his real name, Marvin Van Wey. But that still didn't bring me back to God, because I couldn't get rid of my father's words about God punishing my infant child for my sin.

Then the strangest thing happened. My father got religion and started preaching at me. I couldn't believe it. As a teen, I had prayed for him, now things were turned around. I grew meaner and ruder the more people preached at me. I didn't do it to hurt them, but in order to see if they were different from me. I wanted to know if God could really change hearts. Every one of those people let me down. I could lead each of them to the breaking point where they would sound and act just like one of us heathens.

So, it wasn't a human who told me to go get my Bible on this day, it was Creator Redeemer.

I finally found a Bible in my sons' footlocker. Bringing it outside, I wondered where to start. The book of Genesis? That didn't seem right, but nothing about the Bible seemed especially interesting to me. I had always believed in God as The Creator. It was a natural heritage from my Native American background, but I wasn't convinced he was always good, or that he had time for the likes of me. Surely he was busy doing God things in heaven, otherwise why didn't he do something about the mess down here?

Read the book of John.

I had read the Gospel of John before. It had some nice poetic words I didn't see how applied to my life, but it's hard to argue when God is speaking to you, so I opened the Bible to the Gospel of John and began reading. By the time I finished reading my mind had somehow chosen faith.

These men, these followers of Jesus Christ, had given their lives for what they believed. They had walked and talked with Jesus, who was killed on a cross for claiming to be equal with his father, God. I did not believe these men would all give their lives for a lie.

My mind was opened to things I had never seen before, and I suddenly understood that God wasn't the one who punished my son. It was the first time I realized that a lot of things I had been told about God probably weren't the truth about God.

In the beginning was the Word and the Word was with God, and the Word was God.

Didn't that fit with everything my ancestors believed? It also fit that God became a human, making a way for me to relate with him.

The Word became flesh and lived for a while among us . . . God did not send his Son into the world to condemn the world, but to save the world through him.

I don't know how I missed the meaning of the words before. They rang out like sweet music and opened a longing I hadn't felt for years, but the promise of no condemnation and new life also came with a warning.

Whoever believes in him is not condemned, but whoever does not believe stands condemned already because he has not believed in the name of God's one and only son.

The realization that I was condemned already let me know I had a responsibility to make a choice, but I also knew I had a need for something outside of myself to change the inside of me. Still, months passed before I admitted my longing for God to Cat. I feared he would leave me if he found out I believed in a personal relationship with Creator. My final decision came in a most unusual way.

Cat and I traveled down the hill to attend a special showing of a Johnny Cash movie at our church. It was a surprise to both of us to discover Johnny Cash's deep faith and the fact he didn't claim to be perfect because of it. At the end of the service, the pastor asked people to come forward for prayer at the altar. A feeling came over me that if I would stand up for God then he would stand up for me. What an amazing thought, that the Creator of the universe would stand up for me.

The pastor had everyone close their eyes and sing a familiar song while people made their way to the altar. Cat stoodd on my right. I slipped out of the pew on my left and went forward. When I reached the front, I clenched my eyes shut to keep tears from falling. I honestly thought I was giving up everything, including Cat, to follow Creator. That's how strongly I felt about my decision.

When I opened my eyes, Cat was standing beside me!

We had both stepped out of the pew at the same time going different directions but ending up in the same place. He wrapped my hand in his and, together, we gave our lives to this awesome Creator Redeemer, or at least that's what we thought we were doing. In reality, Cat gave his life completely to the control of God, but I held back, wanting to see results before I gave up too much.

Cat's in-your-face-right-now temper took three steps back until it finally disappeared altogether. The first to witness this change was a man who pushed Cat right to the limit. Cat's enormous hands grabbed the man by the shirt and lifted him off his feet. Cat held him there for several minutes while the man trembled in terror.

"You're lucky," Cat finally said through gritted teeth. "I'm a Christian now, or you'd be picking yourself up in pieces."

Then Cat slowly lowered the quaking mass of a man back to the ground. From that moment on, Cat never allowed his anger to push him to the point of striking or grabbing another human with the intention of doing harm.

My change came more slowly. Fear of losing control of my life kept me back, and there was that question of why God allows pain that kept plaguing me. In the end, it was the goodness of God that drew me closer as I witnessed the transformation in Cat.

October 2009, Between Friday and Saturday
Dad's hospital room

Dad is awake and we are back to watching Rambo movies with the sound turned off. I'm standing next to his bed with my hand on his shoulder so he'll know I'm here. I'm still doing all the talking, but Dad nods in all the right places. I'm actually enjoying this time with him; I've never watched Rambo movies before this hospital stay.

"Watch," I say to Dad, "the girl is going to die. She always does. Somebody should warn her to stay away from that Rambo guy."

The scenes where Rambo runs through the forest have me laughing out loud. The movie makers depict the local Sheriff's department as a bunch of inept bimbos. I'm glad that's not usually the truth in my neck of the woods. Most of our deputies know the forest better than they know their own backyards; they are tough family men like my father, protecting our freedoms. I wouldn't want to be on the wrong side of them. Still, as I watch Rambo wandering around like some kind of wild animal, I cannot help but relate. Sometimes what we call civilization just seems plumb crazy.

When Dad drifts off to sleep, I think back to the wilderness trip Tresa and I took together. The world was going crazy back then too.

16

Whispers and a Roar

This is our most desperate hour.

—*John Eldridge*

September 11, 2001
Sky Lakes Wilderness, Southern Oregon

It is dark when I open my eyes to discover Tresa curled in a ball and asleep on the end of the cot. Checking the hanging clothes, I discover my only two pair of jeans are still soaked from last night's storm, so it'll be a morning of sitting around camp for me. I open the tent flaps to see if the rain has stopped. Strips of pink clouds dot the sky with a faint glow in the east. It's a good sign. I lay a fire in the outside pit and fill the coffeepot with water from the stream. When I return to the tent, Tresa jumps up, raring to go.

"How's the weather?" she asks.

"Hard to tell this early," I answer, "but the clouds seem to have left."

She sticks her head out the door. "Lookin' good. We can string this stuff up outside and it'll dry faster."

"Good idea. You can take care of that while I start the pancakes."

"You planning to use the huckleberries we picked?"

"Yep."

She grins. "How about using a few less than normal. I would appreciate a bit of pancake with my huckleberries."

She has a point. A friend says I'm "full of it," meaning I never do anything half way. I put the griddle on top of the wood stove and smear it with butter. Then I pour a ladle of batter in six circles before I start dotting them with the crimson-colored berries I picked in the patch behind our tent. The sweet aroma soon fills the tent.

Dishing up three pancakes apiece onto two blue spatterware plates lined with paper plates, I get out the peanut butter and jelly. Tresa passes on the jelly and pours syrup over hers. Then we both head out to the fire where we can watch the sunrise. I've already covered two stump rounds with towels so we can sit and enjoy our breakfast.

We eat in silence until Tresa starts laughing.

"What?"

"You should see yourself."

I look down at my tie-dyed purple and red dress. It's more a gigantic tee shirt than anything else, and it's the most comfortable thing I own. I say, "This was supposed to be my nightshirt, but it's the only dry thing I have at the moment."

Tresa shakes her head. "It's not just the dress. I've never seen anyone wearing a hippy headband and a cowboy hat and a holster and a vest and thick wool socks and tennis shoes *with* a dress. You, my friend, are the picture of fashion."

"Who's to see?"

She shrugs and cuts another bite of pancake. I examine her ensemble—a floppy green hat, heavy boots, three layers of shirts, and long underwear showing beneath her jeans. I mumble, "You're one to talk."

She looks down and chuckles. "Who's to see?"

We both chuckle at that. In many ways, we are very different from one another, but in just as many ways, we are very much alike. The same spirit of adventure fills both our hearts, and neither one of us would pass an opportunity to try something new. I certainly didn't have to pressure Tresa to join me on this trip. We both enjoy the fresh aroma of a rain-drenched forest and burning incense cedar, even after the harrowing storm we had last night . . . or maybe it's more accurate to say . . . *because* of it.

Tresa folds her paper plate, tucks it in embers of the fire, and points toward my holster. "Why do you always carry the pistol?"

I look down at my .44 Special. "Better to be safe than sorry."

"I feel safe without," she says.

"Yeah," I say, "I know, but I feel safer with."

"Think it'll stop a bear?"

"Probably not."

"A cougar?"

I think about Marvin Wright. He's one of the oldtimers from Prospect who spent a lifetime hunting mountain lions with his hounds. "You'll never see it coming," he once told me. "That pistol will still be in your holster when the lion sinks its teeth into the back of your neck."

I shudder at the memory of his words.

Tresa's piercing brown eyes stare into mine, waiting for an answer.

"Nope," I say. "It probably wouldn't stop a cougar."

"So, what's it for?"

"People."

She nods. I figure it's the end of the discussion, but she goes on to tell me how she solo hikes hundreds of miles across the Pacific Crest Trail every year and has never felt the need to carry any kind of weapon.

"I know," I say, "but things happen to me."

"Like what?"

"Things." I wash down my last bite of huckleberry pancake with hot coffee. Then I give Tresa my eagle-eye stare. "You've never had the need of a weapon."

She nods.

"I have."

She stares at me for several minutes, then she jumps to her feet and says, "I'm heading to Ranger Springs. It'll be late before I return."

"Fine," I say, "I'm planning to hunt up Gopher Ridge."

It's not really the truth, but it sounds good. I've been hunting for a couple of years now, but I'm not what you would call a serious hunter. I bought my hunting license and tags, and I carry my pistol on my hip and sling a rifle over my shoulder. They're more for protection than anything else. But the image is good, and I like keeping it.

"You planning to wear that getup?" Tresa asks.

I grimace. "I'll be hanging around camp until my clothes dry."

She smiles. "Good idea. Somebody might mistake you for a target."

"Very funny."

But she missed my comment. She's already gathering her gear for a long day's hike. By the time she's ready, I've finished taking stock of our supplies and washing the dishes with heated creek water. I tell her to have a good time and return safe.

"You ruin all my fun," she says. She throws me a wave and flies across our log-turned bridge.

I've never figured out how she gets across that thing without falling into the creek. I'm lucky to maneuver one step at a time with my arms held out to my sides for balance. I watch her go, and then I cut two bushy fir limbs from the underside of a tree and use them to sweep the tarp that serves as a floor in our cabin tent. I love keeping house in a tent. It's easy to keep track of things in this small 12-by-12 space.

By the time I'm finished the sun has risen over the hill. Everything . . . trees, stumps, rocks, the tent, the flag . . . sizzles in the warmth of the sun. Steam rises in giant puffs to the sky. I pull my camouflage coat over my long nightshirt, grab my rifle and head up the bluff behind camp. Frost has hardened the mud, and the going is easy to a far-seeing spot where I can check out storm damage. Light wind blows through my hair. The sky is so blue I feel

I could plunge into it. The air smells of rich earth and spicy plant life. I pull in the scent of it and my heart catches at the smell of wood smoke.

Off in the distance, spiraling drifts of smoke lift into the sky. Counting, I discover 14 fires started by lightning strikes. Most are small, but a couple of the fires are big enough to be threatening. I plan to keep an eye on them as I head back to camp.

My clothes are still wet, so I put another log in the fire pit and pull out a cot from the tent. After setting the cot on a flat place in the warmth of the sun, I lie back and relax. I can't do this at home. There's too many thing to do—too many phone calls; too much work; too many distractions, both good and bad; too much noise; too much commotion; too much of everything. Out here there are few distractions, and I don't feel I have to jump up and do something at any given moment.

On a past camping trip, Cat and I actually watched a gopher pop up out of the hard ground at his feet. We were both sitting in the sun at the time, reading books. Cat whistled, and when I looked, he pointed to the ground. We could hear a small scratching noise. For the next thirty minutes we continued to listen until the little creature clawed his way through. He sniffed the ground in front of him, then turned and sniffed Cat's boot.

Bloop! Back in the ground he went.

We remained completely still, and a few minutes later he popped back out. He made several little scurries around our feet, picking up bits and pieces of dropped food, and then he plopped back into the hole, pulling dirt in behind him. The ground looked no worse for wear. It was as if he had never been there.

Another time, Cat and I watched an ant kill a grasshopper that was about ten times its size.

Just sitting . . . just being . . . is so foreign to my usual world. At home, I often find myself making excuses if Cat finds me sitting for any length of time. But out here, there is no need of excuse. I revel in my solitude and peace, feeling the sun warming my skin. Can I carry this sense of rightness back to the real world? Will I ever learn to say "no," and separate spaces of solitude midst the busyness? I hope so. I pray so. But it usually doesn't take long, after I return home, before the old grind starts burying me.

Perhaps, this time, it will be different.

Thinking of the word *different,* I realize that something feels really different right now. The forest is quieter than usual, but I'm not sure why. The swooshing of the nearby waterfall still meets my ears, camp jays squawk and argue over the leftover pancakes I've spread out for them, and I can hear the wind singing in the tops of the trees, but a prevailing quiet seems extraordinary. I decide it must be because the storm has silenced the bees. Buzzing usually fills the forest. I suspect they will be back before long, mad as all get out, and making their last mark of the season by stinging anyone in their path.

I'm nearly asleep, wondering how far Tresa will venture today, when a terrific rumbling nearly shakes me off my cot.

My first thought is of thunder. The second is of an earthquake. The ground begins to shake and our flag flaps in a sudden burst of wind.

An enormous Air Force bomber appears over the bluff, dropping our camp into shadow. I jump up, ready to run! But the red underbelly tells me it's a borade bomber, sent out by the forest service to smother the largest of the 14 fires.

Dropping to the cot in relief, I clutch my chest and shake my head. Goodness! That was the event of the day. What a shock after such utter silence.

As the echoing rumbles fade through the forest, I realize it really is quiet out here.

One of my biggest pet peeves about the Sky Lakes Wilderness is that the flight plan of all major jet lines in our area goes right over us. I've always been jealous of my friend, Jack Hollenbeak. He was born in 1910 and led most of the crews that cut the trails into this basin. He experienced the wilderness in a way I cannot.

On the other hand . . . when was the last time I heard a plane fly over?

I lie back and look at the sky. There's not a jet stream anywhere.

Perhaps there's a wind up high, washing the skies clean, but our flag is hanging limp and lifeless. There's no wind here. I listen. There's not even the noise of a small single-engine plane. I begin to wonder if the bomber truly is the only plane I've heard all day. Swinging my legs over the side of the cot, I decide to hike up Gopher Ridge. I'll take my rifle so Tresa will think I just went for a hike. But my real reason for climbing up the steep face is to reach a spot where I can contact someone on my cell phone. There's something really odd about no planes being in the sky today.

My jeans are still damp, but I pull them on anyway. I lay my flannel shirt over the wood stove for the briefest of moments before slipping it over my arms. The warmth of it feels good. I pack a quick lunch of a peanut butter sandwich, a granola bar, and an orange. Then I grab my rifle and head out.

Climbing the steep switchbacks of Gopher Ridge is not fun. Huffing and puffing my way up, I stop at the first patch of huckleberries for a free snack. My second stop is at a far-seeing place overlooking the north end of the Sky Lakes Wilderness. Boston Bluff stands far below me now, but a giant hand has painted a white wash over the top of it. The bluff sparkles like an enormous jewel in the sun. Lake Ivern shimmers like a beckoning treasure. I almost decide to head back down, that the trip over the ridge isn't worth it, after all, but then the Borade bomber returns, reminding me of why I'm up here.

Turning and trudging up the trail, I take no more breaks until I'm over the top.

Finding a place to sit in a sun-bathed meadow, I stare over ridge after ridge of glorious wooded mountains. Flounce Rock, the mountain behind my home, stands in the distance. It looks small and un-notable from my high perch, but it holds the tower that will connect me to the rest of the world. Three incoming calls wait unanswered on my phone. My thirteen-year-old granddaughter, Samantha, who lives between San Diego and Los Angeles, is the first I call.

"New York has been attacked," she says.

"No way!"

"I've been watching it on TV all day. The airports are closed and most schools."

The shock of the news takes my words away. Samantha keeps talking as I watch the breeze changing the color of tall grass from green to gold and back again.

Up here, I hear the drone of bees and a dozen different kinds of small insects as they dart around scarlet paintbrush, purple larkspur, mountain bluebells, and golden asters. Black hooded Oregon Juncos beep and babble in the trees. The sweet smell of chokecherries and wildflowers mingle with the aroma of warm fir trees, a combination of Christmas and summer all rolled together. Storm clouds gather in the eastern sky with a hint of winter on its way. A hawk soars freely in the air above me.

The news of an attack seems surreal.

"It's awful," Samantha says. "Thousands of people have died."

Wishing she was sitting beside me instead of over a thousand miles away, I try to find some words of comfort. Then I hang up the phone and call my father. He's the second person on my return-call list.

"It's worse than Pearl Harbor," he says.

Tears well in my eyes. My throat constricts so badly I cannot talk. I've heard myriad stories about the Battle of Pearl Harbor. None of them were good.

A doe feeds in the tall timber to my left. A fawn snuggles in to nurse. I'm wishing my family were all around me, here, where it's safe. I can't stand to think of anything happening to my children and grandchildren. Then I think about all those lives lost in New York City.

The last call I make is to Cat.

"Stay there," he says.

"How can I stay?"

"Stay," Cat urges again. "You can do as much there as you can down here. The President is calling for everyone to pray."

Cat is right. What better place to pray than out here where I can reach out and touch the One who answers prayer.

October 2009, Between Friday and Saturday
Dad's hospital room

Dad is still asleep, so I sit on the bench and think about that awful time on 9/11. On my way to the trailhead for that trek into the wilderness, I stopped at a friend's house to drop off some library books. I had watched the movie, *The Patriot,* the night before and thoroughly loved it. The story was a great depiction of a man who yearned for peace but would do whatever it took to keep his family safe. The main character reminded me of my husband and made me proud to be Cat's wife.

My friend hated the movie. She said, "People were such savages back then. I'm glad we're more civilized."

Her words haunted me after I received news of the terrorist attack. That act was not something I would have called civilized. I remember thinking that surely the world had never seen such evil, but then I remembered Jack Hollenbeak had lived through two world wars.

I thought then, as I think now, that evil has been around a long time. The best way to guard against it is to first take care of my own heart. Through prayer I can work to withstand any root of bitterness, or seed of hate, or anger to take root. It comes down to not allowing myself to indulge in road rage, or shouting matches, or negative talk, or negative think about one of my fellow humans. It comes down to working at bettering the relationships with the people closest to me.

I bow my head and pray.

My relationship with my earthly father seems to be healed, and I am stronger because of it. My relationship with Momma is still in need, but we can begin now in making good memories. What other reason could Creator Redeemer have for taking Dad home to Heaven and leaving Momma behind with me as her only child to watch out for her?

It is more an assurance than a question, and along with it comes the same assurance Dad will not leave this hospital alive. I am saddened at that fact for myself, but glad for Dad. He received a glimpse of Heaven back when he had his first heart attack and he's been homesick for that safe place ever since.

17

Creator Redeemer

Great are you Lord . . .
Our heart is unquiet until it rests in you.

—Saint Augustine

October 18, 2009
Dad's hospital room

Weeks have passed now with me mostly in this hospital beside Dad. My children and grandchildren have all said their goodbyes to their Grandpa. I've spent every night but three here. Momma comes during the day and my Uncle Roy is usually beside her. He started for his home in Southern California twice when Dad's prognosis looked good, but before he even reached the airport in Redding California, he turned around and came back at the news that time was short.

All three of us are in this room with Dad and the doctor right now. It's not a good combination. Our expectations soar high whenever we get a good prognosis from the doctor, then they dip and plummet when the news is bad. I've learned not to listen too much to the doctor. Most of his information is a mere guess at best. He means well, but his resources are limited.

There is a horror that sneaks into the most sacred moments. The three of us have prayed with each other and with Dad, we've said our goodbyes to him, and we've kept our accounts fairly short. Yet we know so little of what comes next. Many harsh words have been exchanged in this room, a lot of them holding the power death.

I sit on the bench now, knitting a prayer shawl. It won't be good for anything. The stitches are all uneven, but the action keeps me quiet so I won't irate my mother. She's losing the most important person in her life. Like the uneven stitches in my shawl, she is all knotted up inside. I'm glad Roy is here to help her.

They are both unhappy with me, because I have ordered this meeting. I did so, because I want to know why my father is being starved. He weighs little more than 130 pounds right now and the respirator is turned up as high as it will go.

I've been awake for two days. Dad has been unable to sleep. I was going to return home today for a nap, but the doctor promised to come answer some of my burning questions. Right now he's wasting valuable time telling us how he's too busy to answer our questions.

My questions are written down. A compassionate, knowledgeable nurse spent last night with me telling me I should do this very thing. When the doctor finishes with his spiel, I begin.

"What is the best we can expect?"

The doctor hems and haws.

I get more specific. "Who made the decision to intubate my father again?"

We were all delighted when the tube was removed and Dad was even able to share a few words with us, but very few, because he was too weak to talk.

I take ten minutes of the doctor's precious time. I timed it with the big wall clock. He took five minutes telling us how he didn't have time. When the doctor leaves, Roy asks Momma if she received the answers to her questions.

"No," she says. "Did you?"

Roy shakes his head. "No, but it was good that Sandra got hers answered."

I'm so sick of the name, Sandra, I could scream. It would make me feel real good right now to have somebody call me Sandy. That's not about to happen, though, because my mouth does not stay shut as it should.

"Why didn't you ask the doctor your questions when he was here," I say a little too loudly.

"I would not waste his time that way," Roy says. "He has a lot of patients."

"Waste his time?" I say. "Dad is one of his patients and has been for over a month. I've barely talked with the doctor this whole month. I don't think asking him questions concerning Dad's life are a waste of time."

"Go home," Roy says. "You're tired."

"No," I say, surprising myself. "I have every bit as much right to be here as you do, and you're tired too."

It's the truth, but I won't stay, because my emotions are taking over. I stuff my shawl into a bag and hurry out, not even saying goodbye to Dad. I feel bad about that, but I'm like a mother on an airplane when the little oxygen masks have fallen down and she knows she must help herself before she can help her child.

I run through the hall and out the door, sobbing all the way. When I get behind the wheel of my Explorer, I don't know what to do.

I sit there for many minutes until I realize I must eat. My brain is no good at all. I head to a local restaurant and sit by myself and stuff food into my mouth that I cannot taste. Tears run down my cheeks for the 20 minutes it takes me to eat. No one looks at me, not even the waiter.

I do not exist.

When I'm fairly sure my glucose levels are safe enough to drive, I head for the hills. Several times, I feel myself drifting off to sleep. I just cannot stay awake. When I reach Eagle Point and stop for a traffic signal, I see a full rainbow stretched in the sky before me.

That rainbow is a promise from Creator Redeemer to all of us, but right now it is a special promise to me.

Twice I've had a rainbow fall into my lap. I was driving down the road near our house one day while watching a rainbow on the hillside next to me. It seemed to be coming closer and closer, which surprised me, because when I was a child chasing rainbows, the end was always elusive. But this time, when I turned a corner, instead of the rainbow drawing further away, it fell right into my lap. It was as if I was swimming in colored air. I didn't even know such a thing was possible. Both experiences happened during a very dark time in my life when I needed assurance of God's love.

This rainbow in front of me now does not fall into my lap, but the beauty of it touches my soul, and once again assures me of my Heavenly Father's love. I pull out my cell phone and ask my friend, Lynn, if I can stop for a hug. I've never before placed such a request before anyone other than my husband. She says, "Yes," and I take her up on it, getting needed rest, as well, for the trip home. It feels good to have someone care about me.

It is early evening when I pull into my driveway, and I'm asleep as fast as I hit the bed. I sleep through the night and all of the next day. Then I wake with a start.

It's time.

After pulling my legs over the side of the bed, I hurry and dress for a return to the hospital. Creator Redeemer is talking with me while I move through my house.

Your father loves you, but he's coming home to me now.

Somehow, I understand my father's passing will not leave me without a father's love. Creator Redeemer has always held the highest place of a father in my life, though I didn't always recognize it. He is the One who is always faithful, even when I am faithless.

Slow down.

Even as I hear the words, I know God doesn't expect me to slow down in getting dressed for the hospital. He means for me to slow my *life* down.

Take a sabbatical.

I pull out my phone and call Lynn, my friend and co-teacher. When she answers, I say, "You are my witness, Lynn, don't let anybody talk me out of this. I'm not teaching for a year."

She says something about waiting till later, after I'm not so emotional, to make such a decision, but I am adamant and she finally agrees to hold me to it.

When I hang up, the phone rings. "Better get here fast as you can," a nurse says."

I'm already out the door. The words of Chris Rice's Untitled Hymn (Come to Jesus) are playing on my iPod as they have been for the past two weeks, and I think of the movie, *Big Fish,* that I recently watched.

When I reach the hospital, I run down the hall. A wall of nurses and technicians surround my father, but I push through them all and grab Dad's hand.

"Dad," I say. "We're gonna break outta here!"

The tube is gone again, and Dad's eyes open wide as he starts to sit up. The group of medical personnel looks at me with startled eyes. I think they believe they are seeing a down-to-earth miracle.

I lower my voice in an effort to sound conspiratorial. "Not yet, Dad. We have to wait for all these medical people to leave. And of course we'll need Clay to help you out of that bed."

Our youngest son, Clay, is nearly six-foot-seven, a big guy. I can see by Dad's delighted expression that he understands we need "The Big Guy."

Of course, I know Dad will not leave this place with me, but I also know he is going to break away and bust outta here. I've told Roy several times that when you've seen God, everything else turns to shadow in comparison, and Dad has seen God. He's ready to go.

Fifteen minutes later, Clay emerges through the door and, with a big smile, Dad says clearly, "The Big Guy!"

Clay doesn't know what to think. He doesn't yet know the story behind the words, but he gives Dad a strong man's hug and it's the last one he'll get on this side of glory.

Dad's body does not die tonight, but it is the last night he will ever speak with us. At one point, when I step out of his view, Dad calls very loudly, "Where's my daughter?"

"He's been saying that ever since the tube was removed," my mother says.

Her voice is tired and worn. I wish I could give her a big hug, but the chasm between us is to deep right now. I comfort myself with the knowledge that we will soon work on spanning that chasm. For now, it is enough to have Roy here to take care of my mother's needs.

"I'm right here, Dad," I assure him, and I praise Creator Redeemer that my father does indeed have his daughter right here beside him all the way to the time when he will pass through the shadow of death and fly away to Jesus.

18

Safe Arrival

And with your final heartbeat
Kiss the world goodbye
Then go in peace, and laugh on Glory's side.

—*Chris Rice*

October 22, 2009, the last day
Dad's hospital room

Dad left for Heaven early this morning. Momma and Roy were on one side of his bed and I was on the other. Momma held his right hand while I held his left. I held his hand until I felt the warmth go out of it.

When he took his last breath, I looked up at the ceiling and said, "See ya soon Dad. Save a place for me."

I could almost hear his laughter, but when I looked back at his body, I saw nothing but an empty shell. Roy took Momma home while I was left to take care of the paperwork regarding Dad's body.

Now, I'm home, alone, and Cat is on the phone asking me to join him at base camp this evening.

"No," I say.

Cat does not accept that answer, so I climb back into my Ford Explorer and drive up the winding road to Bessie Camp Shelter in the foothills of the High Cascades. I don't allow myself to think. I simply listen to worship songs and remind myself that Creator Redeemer is still with me.

At base camp, Steve Evans feeds me a meal fit for a woodsman. I sit and listen to the hunting talk over the sizzle of the wood camp stove and life seems almost normal. The air is filled with friendly smells . . . roasted meat, horse sweat and wood smoke.

When I finish my meal, I take my leftovers outside to share with Red Dog. Temperatures have dropped to below freezing, causing moonlight to sparkle off frosted trees. It's as if a thousand angels are keeping watch over us. Crunching steps nearing from behind cause me to hold my breath, but when I turn to look it's nothing to be afraid of, it's only a deer.

It's hard to shake off the feeling that time has stopped, that the people in this base camp are the only humans who exist in the entire world. The feeling stays with me until I spot a fast moving light in the sky. At first it makes a silent track, but soon the rumble of a jet reaches my ears. I imagine the people sitting in the jet, bored, trying to sleep, and frustrated at having to travel at night. Do they imagine me down here in the middle of this forest?

I think not. Most of them have forgotten the wilderness.

I hear the mournful song of a single coyote wailing out his frustration. Perhaps he missed dinner. I wonder if God hears—if he will bring an ailing rabbit running along in front of the coyote?

I hunt for the lioness, the book of Job says, *I count the months till the doe bears her fawn.*

Thinking of Job reminds me that not everything goes perfectly in this world, but for those of us who accept Creator Redeemer's gift of life, there is hope even in the most dark of circumstances. In the beginning God created; now he redeems and recreates.

A future and hope.

Cat wraps his arms around me. As usual, I didn't hear his approach. He whispers in my ear, letting me know that he understands and loves me for who I am—a woman who loves the wilderness and all things wild. Here, where the wild animals roam, is a safe place for me.

Wilderness, by description is a place untamed and untouched by humans—a place that clearly carries the mark of Creator Redeemer. Yet God's touch can be found anywhere, from a rainbow spanning the heavens over a great metropolis to a tiny bird nest hanging on a cliff . . . even in a dying father's hospital room while his daughter watches over him and waits for him to speak his love to her. The words never came, as I watched over my father, but the touch did, and the touch spoke louder than any words.

Epilogue

Whoever is wise, let him heed these things
and consider the great love of the LORD.

—Creator Redeemer

March 23, 2011
Aspen Cabin, Box R Ranch

Honking geese wake me this morning as they welcome
the sunrise. I'm tucked away in a log cabin at Box R Ranch
above Ashland, Oregon. I come here often when snow
blankets the forest and I need a warm refuge in the womb
of the mountain.

Cat joins me after work in the evenings, and we soak
up the smell and life of each other before an open fireplace.
The aroma of burning pine and cedar fills our lungs. Then
he leaves each morning, heading to the valley, while I pour
my life into a stream of words.

I came here to finish the writing of this story with as few
distractions as possible. No phone, no TV, and no people
talk. I've moved my laptop from room to room, sitting on
an overstuffed couch in front of a stone fireplace, to a table
near a window overlooking a small lake and tree-shrouded
meadow, to the upstairs loft where rain song is loudest.

At the writing of this book, it's been nearly two years since Dad left for Heaven. A lot of changes have taken place in that time.

I miss my father. Several times, I broke down in great heaving sobs while writing this book. If given the chance to relive my life I would choose to enjoy my father more and worry about my feelings less. I would choose to believe my father loved me and respond in kind.

Love really is a choice, and we can choose it, especially with Creator Redeemer's help.

I've made that choice of love with my mother; choosing to believe she loves me even when her actions speak the opposite. In making that choice, I finally have the mother I always wanted, at least most of the time. And at last we have good memories for each of us to cherish . . . sharing tacos across a table; gathering tomatoes and green beans from the garden that Momma calls Cat's weed patch; crying together over sad movies; cheering for the winners of a television game show; filling in the words of a crossword puzzle; laughing over the antics of Chester, Momma's dachshund and faithful companion; praying for my Uncle Roy who has been courageously battling throat cancer.

I hope Momma lives forever, but of course, that will not happen in this world. However, I am thankful for the hope of Heaven together forever. It is a very sure and real hope. My only regret is that we didn't try to mend our relationship sooner.

Momma and I have both undergone changes. That's what relationships are all about. There is no fifty-fifty deal here; it's giving a hundred percent from both sides. Both of us have given, and both of us have received. I've given time and a listening ear. In return Momma has attempted to answer some of my most difficult questions, in spite of the fact it made her very uncomfortable to do so.

I've discovered our issues aren't nearly as personal as I first thought.

I thought there was something lacking in my personality that only my mother could see. Such thinking made me afraid to allow others into my life, because I assumed that in time they would see whatever it was my mother saw and reject me. The truth is that I simply did not fill the role my mother had picked out for me.

Most of us laugh when we see these role expectations and clashes in movies. *Driving Miss Daisy* is a great example. So why is it that the same expectations and clashes become so serious when our own lives are involved?

One winter, long ago, I became so discouraged and frustrated with life that I jumped in my car and drove down to Gold Ray Dam to throw myself into the Rogue River.

After parking at the top of the dam, I didn't even get out of the car. The roar of water was incredibly loud. The river poured over the dam in a spray of white foam that looked like some kind of monster. So I drove on down to a calmer section of the river before walking into the water and heading to the other side. I planned to keep moving until the current pulled me under and away, but the river never rose above waist deep. I made it across and back and all I did was get cold and wet.

I didn't discover till later that walking across the river in that section was an utter impossibility. My Native friends call it my River Walk, because they believe Creator changed the river just for me. I've come to agreement with them.

Thinking about the river episode now makes me chuckle. Although I had thought I was discouraged and frustrated enough at the time to take my life, the real truth was that I was simply discouraged and frustrated. I didn't really want to die. If I had, I would have jumped in at the dam. Either way, I'm very glad now to be alive. True. I may have saved myself some pain in the long run if I had taken my life that day, but I would have missed out on a whole lot of joy.

There is sanctity of life that is worth preserving. I think that's why death makes us so sad.

Many old friends have already left this world. My hunting partners, Mike Calderwood and Gary Shaw have both joined Creator Redeemer. Gary died in his sleep. It was shocking news. Gary was one of the most alive people I've ever known. Every time I think of him, I see his enormous smile. Over 700 friends filled the church for his memorial service. Many more of us would have been there if the news had reached us in time. I'm sad for his family. But I'm not sad for Gary. He lived his adventure well and was totally ready to meet Creator Redeemer face-to-face.

I keep imagining Gary going to bed, thinking he would face another day of work in the morning, probably thinking about some of the problems and deadlines needing fixed, but instead, he wakes to the wonderful face of God.

Goodness.

As Robert Frost said, "One could do worse than being a swinger of branches."

I want all my branches to take me closer to God.

Even as I think the thought I hear the wail of a coyote. Though my feet are bare, I run to the porch where I breathe in air so clean my lungs fill to bursting with the cold of it. The geese fall silent as the lone coyote continues his plaintive howl. It's that time between times when the night animals make their way to bed while the rest of us welcome the dawn.

Last night I wrote the last words of my story, knowing it is but a chapter, though an important one. After closing my laptop, I pulled on my boots and hurried outside. It was as if someone had called my name. And there, in the meadow below Aspin cabin, a herd of elk rummaged through the grass. When the last one disappeared into the forest, a bull elk began his bugle, a love song echoing through the forest and across the meadow for many minutes.

I accepted it for what it was—a gift from Creator Redeemer, an acknowledgement of his presence and grace that is always with me making every place a safe place.

This daughter's search for a father's love is at long last stilled. My discovery is that Creator Redeemer offers the ultimate father love that can never be taken away, and I've known His love from the first moment I roamed through the forest as carefree and fearless as any wild animal.

I've been accused of being a rebel, but I'm not really. It's simply the call of the wild runs deep in my blood. I hear it every time I smell the musky scent of game and wet earth. I savor it over open fires and far-seeing places, and I dream of it on my bed at night when the rain makes music on the roof and I begin planning the next adventure.

Wild is more than a physical untamed place, it's an unrestrained soul soaring on the wings of the wind. It is a connection to the heart of Creator Redeemer—a total immersion in a Father's love.

Acknowledgments

Wild Woman was a lifetime in the living and over a decade in the writing. My biggest fear is that I will forget to acknowledge someone who was absolutely essential to the story.

In a way, everyone who has ever touched my life is a part of this story. Even as you read this, your story becomes a part of mine, and mine becomes a part of yours . . . a part of Creator Redeemer's story as he planned it before ever a word was formed on any of our tongues. The story is about relationship, first with Him, and then with each other.

Please forgive me if your name is not on this list and should have been. I probably thought of you in the middle of the night *after* the book went to press. Please know that you are appreciated and will one day be rewarded from the One who never forgets.

A special thanks to Marlene Bagnull for being the first published writer to encourage me as a scribe. Her encouragement spurs me on to this day and, for many years now, we've been sharing the elk/wapiti adventure together, making tracks across the vast Colorado wilderness.

William Watkins, my first agent, was the first to believe in this story, telling me, rightfully, that it should be the first book I publish. Lawrence Jordan, my second agent, stole the pages from my open book bag and refused to give them back. Later, he called from New York City to tell me I needed to head into the wilderness and seek Creator Redeemer for the "real" story. Every time the man calls me, wisdom pours through the phone. I also owe him special thanks for walking me through the faith process when Cat and I nearly lost our current forest home.

My Chiloquin native friends, Buttons and Diana Shadley, and Don and Mary Gentry encouraged me with deep felt prayers through my dark hour of the soul when I lost sight of the vision. Terry Pruitt and Ryan Clark prayed me through what it meant to "restore the foundation and rebuild the walls."

Fabulous authors, Wanda Dyson and Robert Liparulo pushed me to the finish line, cheering all the way. They walk the talk and, for the record, Wanda is the best wapiti finder/driver on the face of this planet. She is my first choice on a photo shoot.

Lonnie Hull DuPont, Steve Barclift, and Cindy Lambert for encouragement in the early stages. Phil Lemons for always being there in prayer (and with mandolin).

Pastors Russ Rea, John Courson and Rick Booye for giving me a sure foundation.

Steve Evans and Wayne Marshall for the amazing wilderness opportunities and the rest of the guys of Crazy Cyuse and 4E Guide and Supply: Ron Adams, Mike Kaizer, André ,Doug, Robert, Mike, Ken, Ron, Aaron, Eddie, Les, Jeff and others.

Dan Crockett and Jan Brocci of *Rocky Mountain Elk Foundation* for encouraging me in my first hunt. Cristy Rein of *Oregon Fish and Wildlife Journal* for hounding me for more wild stories. Cam Ghostkeeper for writing stories that stirred up my own writing gift.

Tresa Finchum for sharing in my wild adventures, including Wild Woman Chili and Tuna Gravy Glop. I haven't been able to eat a bite of tuna since. The rest of my wild women: Janis Rubus, Karen Reeves, Carrie, Jen Lee, Brooke Snelling, Sharon Weisner, Christie, Ada Hodges,

Julie Krebs, Edie Palmer, Norma Cobb, Amy Dickson and her dog Paden who kept us all warm one snowy night at Alta Lake.

My hunting partners: Bruce Brown, Mike Calderwood, Gary Shaw and Cam Sturm. My river partners: Gary and Nancy Shaw and John and Gail Johnston.

Jim Anderson, neighbor extraordinaire, who shares my love of the outdoors and came to my rescue more times than I can count.

Chris Smith of Wilderness Trails, and his father, Jack, for giving at-risk kids an opportunity to connect with Creator Redeemer in the great outdoors.

Don and Jean Rowlette and Mark and Jeanne Randall for making a place of refuge available at the Greensprings Box R Ranch.

Proofreaders Lynn Leissler, Elsie Dodge, and Marjorie Vawter. Lynn devoted one entire weekend to seeing me through to enering this story in the Westbow/Women of Faith writing contest. My Internet went down and Lynn came to the rescue by hitting the "send" button at the very last possible minute to enter the contest. *Wild Woman* made the finals even though the copy Lynn sent was not the finished manuscript. It's because of Lynn's perseverance you are now reading these words. Marjorie was gracious enough to be my final proofreader and has also become on of my favoirte elk photo drivers. Who would have guessed the woman is such a maniac behind the wheel? She is a master at keeping an eye on the road and another on the critter I'm after while keeping her passengers relatively safe. Elsie caught everything that everybody else missed in spite of become totally immersed in the story. I love your comments such as, "Glory woman, you're hitting mighty close to my memories of Daddy's death," and "Good heavens, I've been so engrossed with this that it's an hour past suppertime! The dog is frantic, and my blood sugar is wavering!" What an encourager you are Elsie!

Rogue Riters, Writers of the Way, and the rest of the crew: Lynn Leissler, Jinny Sherman, John Wiuff, Kristen Parr, Garret Harrington, Nate Bailey, Daniel, Peggy Dover,

Patti Iverson, DJ Note, Maxine Marsolini, Lorrie Benton, Karen Ball, Connie Hull, Andi Smith, Linda & Drennon Carlyle, Betty Lore and Val Coleman. Oregon and Colorado Christian Writers who walked the writing journey with me: Pat Rushford, Sue Miholer, Stan Baldwin, Debbie Hedstrom, Bonnie Leon, Lauraine Snelling, Sandy Dengler, and Jeannie St. John Taylor. Janet Hulstrand for her superb editing on portions of this book.

Garret Harrington for the great cover art and for his amazing support over the years. Debbie Rempel for sharing her expressive poetry and allowing me to put her words to music. Robyn for turning to Creator Redeemer in the midst of her pain . . . and for sharing the words that have become my favorite song.

I'll never forget the canoe ride with Sue Roa as she shared her feelings after reading a first draft of *Wild Woman*. What a great encouragement she was to me. A second thanks to Lynn Leissler, my road trip partner and adventurer, who went the extra mile in reading and re-reading and editing and....

My family who won't be able to read this story for years because of the pain of losing Dad all over again. Thanks to all of you for putting up with your weird Mom and Grandma and Mother-in law.

Dad for giving me a spirit of wild adventure. Momma for hanging in there in prayer even when she didn't agree with my actions.

Cat . . . without him there would be no story.

Creator Redeemer, who wrote the story with His own blood upon the pages of my heart.

Quotation References

Opening: "On His Wings" (original song)
Part One: "If You Could Hear His Voice" (original song)
Chapter One: "I'm His Sheep Walking" (original song)
Chapter Two: Job 38:12
Chapter Three: *The Song of the Little Hunter*
Chapter Four: "Untitled Hymn (Come To Jesus)"

Part Two: "Give Me The Valley" (original song)
Chapter Five: *One Man's Meat*
Chapter Six: "What Susan Said"
Chapter Seven: *Journey of the Magi*
Chapter Eight: British Clergyman and writer (1608-1661)
Chapter Nine: a radio sermon

Part Three: Psalm 50:9-11
Chapter Ten: Psalm 137:1-3
Chapter Eleven: Applegate Christian Fellowship sermon
Chapter Twelve: Jeremiah 29:11
Chapter Thirteen: 2009 Wiconi Family Camp
Chapter Fourteen: Psalm 84:3

Part Four: Job 39:5-8
Chapter Fifteen: Psalm 53:5
Chapter Sixteen: *Waking the Dead*
Chapter Seventeen: *St. Augustine's Confessions*
Chapter Eighteen: "Untitled Hymn (Come to Jesus)"
Epilogue: Psalm 107:43

Contact

Sandy loves hearing from her readers.
You can find her at:
www.sandycathcartauthor.com
www.sandycathcart.com
www.needlerockpress.com
or on Facebook:
Sandy Cathcart Author

Made in the
USA
Lexington, KY